] M000296638

Reading *Reclaimed* is like sitting down with Gina Stinson over pie and coffee for a girlfriend chat. Heartwarming, humorous, hopeful. While each story points to God's faithfulness, Gina's not shy about telling stories on herself about heartaches, heartbreaks and what might have been. Her vulnerability adds a dimension of authenticity, and everyone can find themselves in at least one of the sixty devotions. Pick up one for a friend and leave one on your own bedside table.

—**Letitia Suk,** author of 100 Need-to-Know Tips for Moms of Teens, Author, Speaker, Life Coach

As I read Gina's reflections, I felt a blanket of peace cover me. Yes, we live in a world of trouble, but turmoil can be reclaimed for good, when God is given full access to our pain. I laughed when the dog had gas and cried with the heavy thickness of death. Gina has a way with words that brings poignant understanding to underlying truths. Her clarion call of "More of him, less of me" is one I will seek, too!

—**Sally Ferguson,** author & speaker at sallyferguson.net

It is my pleasure to endorse *Reclaimed* by Gina Stinson. Through her devotional stories, she gives us a peek inside her ministry, life, and family. She doesn't hide her personal struggles and brings the reader to think deeply on many issues including relationships, forgiveness, and loss. Through all of the joys and sorrows, she has learned to place herself in the Potter's hands. Gina allowed herself to reveal her humanity despite the common perception that people in ministry don't have the same hurts and failures that plague others. In her sharing of personal stories, she teaches the value of friendship, choosing wisely, and how to find joy. Most important, when disappointments come, she teaches the reader to find hope in the One who loves us best!

—**Mary E Herman,** Department Chair Elementary Education Department Baptist Bible College 1971–2002, BBFI teaching missionary, 2002 to present

Gina Stinson is one of my hilarity-and-hope sisters. She writes with a blend of humor and transparency that makes spiritual truths somehow seem more attainable in our everyday lives. Her book, *Reclaimed*, shows us how Jesus salvages us from our disasters and performs the ultimate fixer-upper in our lives.

—**Rhonda Rhea,** TV personality, humor columnist, and author of eighteen books, including the award-winning rom-coms, Turtles in the Road and Off-Script & Over-Caffeinated

Full of candor, real life accountings, and a straight-line invitation to the loving care of Jesus, *Reclaimed* is a beautiful collection of stories from Gina's life experiences. With delightful transparency, the reader is encouraged to allow God to reach into their life and rescue them regardless of their need. Through an assortment of relatable situations, we are challenged to trust and allow our own encounter with God to unfold. These writings are exactly what we need in a time where the world stage is full of uncertainty, confusion, unknowns, fears, and challenges. Thank you, Gina, for speaking to our hearts by sharing yours, inviting hope, and setting a foundation for growth as we make our own journey.

—**Pamela McMichen,** MS, EdS, LPC; Licensed Professional Counseling, State of Georgia; Crossway Counseling Center, LLC, Owner/Founder

Sharing practical stories and lessons in her devotional book, *Reclaimed*, Gina writes with personal insight into the ways of God that readers will find easy to understand and relate to. Reading her writing is as comfortable and authentic as conversing with a good friend at a coffee shop.

—**Lori Moody,** Women's Ministry Leadership Team of the Southern Baptist of Texas Convention, Double Honor Ministries Facilitator

In her light-hearted writing style, Gina draws us into her stories and paints memorable pictures that point us to Jesus, the one who responds, rescues, and restores. Her gentle reminders of God's presence offer hope in times of uncertainty and challenge. They highlight the path to reclaiming joy and peace and show us that it's possible to live life to the full. If you're a mess or in a mess right now, I recommend reading *Reclaimed*. It's sure to give you a good dose of encouragement and maybe even a smile.

> **—Twila Belk,** a writer and speaker who loves bragging on God; author of eight books, including The Power to Be: Be Still, Be Grateful, Be Strong, Be Courageous

Gina Stinson's personal, heart-touching, and inspiring stories bring to life the Gospel as it has played out in her existence. In an age of disposable things, Gina reminds us that God never made disposable people. We were all created on purpose and to be loved by our heavenly Father. When we feel defeated, discouraged, or depressed, it helps to have a friend to lift us up out of the hole we've found ourselves in. Gina's words lift us up and help us to imagine the possibilities of redeemed living in Christ. *Reclaimed* will show you the path from the refuse pile of life to the kind of life you can only live through the power and grace of God.

> **—Jason Burden,** 1st Vice President of the BGCT, Senior Pastor, FBC Nederland, Texas

Gina Stinson

reclaimed

The Stories of Rescued Moments and Days

STORYTELLER
PRESS

Reclaimed: The Stories of Rescued Moments and Days
Copyright ©2020 by Gina M. Stinson

ISBN: 978-1-7356402-0-4

Published by Storyteller Press
Winnie, Texas 77665
www.ginastinson.com/books

Interior and Cover Design by Michelle Rayburn
www.missionsandmedia.com

Graphics designed by Savannah Stinson AKA Savannah Scribbles
www.instagram.com/savannahscribbles/

Edited by Stephenie Hovland
www.stepheniehovland.com

Printed in the United State of America 2020—First Edition

Dedication

This book is dedicated to Pop,
who, at the appointed time in history,
found my mom, claimed her for his own,
and inherited me as a feisty stepdaughter.
This bonus dad reached out in love and fathered me
through some of the most difficult times in my life—
sometimes with words,
but most often with his presence.
His presence is a comfort.
Pop isn't ordinary.
He's extraordinary, with large laughs and a big heart.
My only regret is, I wish I'd met him sooner in life.
It is with great appreciation and admiration
for all you have done for my family and me
that this book is lovingly dedicated to you,
Harley T. Morris
Thank you for reclaiming me.

Table of Contents

Introduction

Everybody has a hero—someone who has rescued them from the fire, the hard times, the mess. I can think of a few heroes myself. My parents, a friend or two, my husband, and even my kids have all helped rescue me.

On an early spring morning a few years ago, I needed a rescue. After driving my daughter to meet up with a few friends for the day, I was headed back to our country home about twenty miles from town. It stormed the night before and since I had noticed tree limbs all over the roads as I navigated to town earlier, I decided to take an alternate route home.

I left the safety of our farm to market country road and turned down the county roads, narrow and potholed. It didn't take long for me to realize I had not chosen wisely. After a few miles I came across the first tree across the road. Carefully, I navigated around it, but wasn't too far up the road before I saw the next roadblock. This time the tree was significantly bigger and covered the entire road. Slowly, easing off the brake, I began the very careful crossing of the tree. I got my front tires across the trunk when the road gave a little. I had driven too close to the edge of the road, and the soggy ground crumbled under some of the tired and broken asphalt.

Before I knew what was happening, my car and I were lying at a near ninety-degree angle. I stared at the water-filled ditch to my left and looked to the sky from my right, too scared to move, for fear it would rock the car to the point of flipping. If I ever needed a rescuer, it was that moment. There were no houses in sight. There was no traffic on the country road.

I was left with the only option I had—call my husband. I wasn't sure if I would be greeted with, "What in the world?" "How did you do this?" "Are you OK?" or "Don't worry. I love you." As I waited for him to get there, all I could think about was how glad I was that he was on his way. The rescuer was coming. He could get me out of this mess. He would get our car upright. He would make it all better.

Friends, that's what Jesus does for us. He already knows how we got ourselves into our emergency rescue situation but loves us anyway. He reclaims us, wipes the dust off our feet and gets us upright. His presence is calming, reassuring and confident. Even when it's our own fault, he responds.

As you read these devotions, be encouraged, knowing we've already been rescued. Jesus has given his life for yours. If you know him, then you've been rescued and claimed. But maybe you're like me, and somewhere along the way you discarded important truths and began believing the lies that the world and the enemy fed you. May this be your wake-up call to reclaim all the abundance that God has for you! Your life can be reclaimed for God's glory. Whether you're in a mess because of you, or because of circumstances beyond your control, there is hope, joy, peace, and life waiting to be reclaimed and lived.

Let's do this together. Let's reclaim the promises of God. Let's dig deep and believe what the rescuer and restorer says. He's worth trusting.

Reclaiming every day,

Gina

How to Use This Book

Reclaimed was written as a weekday devotional book. Use *Reclaimed* Monday through Friday as your daily reflection time with the Lord. The easy to read, concise chapters make excellent quick jumpstarts to thinking differently about the moments and days God has given you. With 60 devotions, on a Monday – Friday schedule, *Reclaimed* is a twelve-week study.

Each day you'll read the devotion. The devotions are light-hearted and filled with true stories, but don't let that fool you. Each devotion has a strong rescue message for you to grasp.

The **Stop and Reclaim** section includes the scripture passages used in the devotions and other verses that will reinforce each story. This is the most important part of the book. This is what will change you. The scripture is written out for you so that you can easily use this as an on the go devotional. Take time to sit and think about the scripture before going to the next section.

Take a few moments to journal your thoughts in the **Reclaim Today** section. The topics of forgiveness, grief, and heartache can be heavy. Take your time to be honest and transparent before the Lord. He will help reclaim those moments you've lost.

At the end of the book there are sixty short activities that you can do in approximately one minute. These activities are designed to help you see that reclaiming the lost moments and days begins with little things. Just a minute or two a day, focused on one of these suggestions, can make a difference in how you feel, respond, and navigate through your day.

Enjoy, grow, and reclaim!

Sunshine

$\mathcal{I}$ was seven years old the first time I saw her. We were on our way to Winn Dixie, our local grocery store, when there, among the kudzu draped trees, she popped her head up. My brother, sister, and I did not miss it. Her gray curly hair, her cute disheveled look, the way she stuck her head out of the tangled vines every time a car passed by. How could we not stop and check her out?

But in responsible parent fashion, my mom said, "Let's wait and see if she's still there after we finish at the store, and if she is, we will see about getting her."

I remember the feelings of excitement building. Maybe, just maybe, I would finally have a dog—a pet of my own—a real, live, beautiful poodle-ish, terrier-looking dog. To my delight, my mom returned later that day and picked up the scrawny-looking dog I would later name Sunshine. Unfortunately, the days ahead would prove challenging and tiresome.

Sunshine had to learn how to live civilly. She had to stay in the fence, bark less, and learn to eat out of a bowl instead of the trash can. Her days of street living and stray roaming were over. She had found a home where she was loved, welcomed, and accepted. We thought she was beautiful, but truth be told, this mutt was just about the ugliest I've ever seen. Beauty truly is in the eyes of the beholder. For thirteen years our beloved Sunshine guarded our home. As the years went by, she settled down, moved inside, and was cared for in royal fashion. Patiently enduring numerous cats and other dogs we brought home, she loved us, and we loved her until her final day.

> You've been reclaimed
> for a beautiful purpose.
> You've been rescued.

As I think back to my first understanding of what being rescued or reclaimed looks like, I think of Sunshine. There she was, not even realizing she needed rescuing—popping her head out from the overgrown weeds, looking around, not knowing where her next meal would come from. We picked her up and cleaned her up. She found love and care and food. We thought she was the most beautiful creature ever created. She belonged to our family. She found home or maybe, home found her.

My heart flutters a little as I look at those words: cleaned, fed, loved, beautiful, belonging, family, home. Isn't that a glorious picture of what God has done for us? He has taken me in, rescued me, taken away the title of "stray" and given me a home, cleaned me up, fed me, loved me unconditionally, called me beautiful, given me his family. That's a beautiful rescue story.

Do you need rescuing today? You are loved more than you can imagine by a Father who sent his Son to take all those distressed situations, bad decisions, sinful choices, and missteps, and turn them into a beautiful story of redemption. You've been reclaimed for a beautiful purpose. You've been rescued. Just like Sunshine.

Stop and Reclaim

So then you are no longer strangers and aliens, but you are fellow citizens with the saints and members of the household of God. (Ephesians 2:19)

Reclaim Today

How has God rescued you?

_____

_____

_____

_____

_____

_____

_____

_____

_____

_____

_____

_____

_____

The Pie Safe

When I was growing up, my mom was the master at taking old things and making them look surprisingly beautiful. She was savvy enough to recover couch cushions, make curtains, and pick up good, used, discarded furniture off the side of the road. Occasionally, she saved enough money to splurge on a treasure at the flea market or a garage sale. She was always on the hunt for a bargain.

On one particular Saturday, I remember her leaving the house with friends to do some secondhand shopping. They didn't have to venture far before my mom had her eyes on a primitive antique pie safe. The dark cherry stained wood, cracked plexiglass (obviously a newer addition to the piece), flat plywood top, and plain legs grabbed her attention. The price tag? One hundred hard-earned dollars.

My mom walked away from the pie safe that day. I remember her coming home and talking about it. She was contemplating the wisdom of her decision. It wasn't two days until she marched herself back to that sale. With a relieved heart, she saw the pie safe (in all its cracked plexiglass glory) had not been purchased. There it was, ready to be reclaimed.

When she brought the pie safe home, she wiped it down with Murphy's Oil and Old English, her favorite furniture polishes. After it was clean, she began the process of deciding where this lovely piece was going to live. And the possibilities were endless. With three shelves, generously spaced, it could be just about anything.

> The possibilities are endless when placed in the hands of the Master Reclaimer.

And over the years, it had so many lives: bookcase, dish cabinet, towel and linen storage, toy storage, trinket display, music cabinet and more. Now, forty years later, the pie safe sits in my bedroom, holding Bibles and treasured books from my collection. It's been reclaimed over and over.

The pie safe is not without scars, but it is useful. It serves a purpose. It's functional. It has its quirks. The door doesn't open as easily as it used to and if you are going to move it, you must handle it with some care. Overall, though, it's still has some life left in it. I doubt my mom had any idea it would last so long. Her investment of one hundred dollars was definitely worth it.

God uses scarred people. He cleans them up and wipes them down. No matter your age, your past, your scars, he can make you useful again. When he reclaims, you have renewed purpose and worth. The possibilities are endless when placed in the hands of the Master Reclaimer.

Stop and Reclaim

For we are his workmanship, created in Christ Jesus for good works, which God prepared beforehand, that we should walk in them. (Ephesians 2:10)

Reclaim Today

Which of your scars is God using to create his masterpiece?

_____

_____

_____

_____

_____

_____

_____

_____

_____

_____

_____

_____

Sixth-Grade Rejection

I remember the first time I faced rejection. I was in the sixth grade and in the most awkward time of my life. I wore large glasses, had crooked teeth, and my mom had just given me permission to decide for myself how the hairdresser would cut my hair.

I chose poorly.

For some reason all these factors did not play a negative part in my confidence. After a few weeks of school under my belt, I began my quest to impress him, a pale-faced, skinny boy in my class. My mission was simple: feed him. The school we attended had cookies for sale, in packages of two, wrapped neatly in aluminum foil. My goal was to buy him a package of cookies each day, drop them off at his desk when he wasn't looking, and let fate have its way with our relationship. I pictured it playing out in slow motion, with him running to me on the playground, thanking me for the cookies and then opening up the package and sharing one with me. It would be a memory we would cherish forever.

Unfortunately, instead, for months he ate the cookies at his desk during lunchtime. He didn't even act like he was interested in finding out who the cookies were from. As time passed, I was getting weary of his disinterest. I was also getting scared I would be caught stealing money out of the change cup from the kitchen cabinet each morning. Five dollars a month was a lot to an unemployed, guilt-ridden, sixth-grade thief.

Finally, one day someone saw me put the cookies on his desk and asked him if he liked me. His response was deafening, even though he whispered, "No, but I like the cookies." He snickered with his informant. I was crushed.

It had been months. Each morning I had risked being caught as I stole the money. Each day I ordered the cookies from the lunch menu. Each lunch period I waited for him to go to the bathroom or get a drink so I could hurriedly place the cookies on his desk and get back to my own desk, so he wouldn't know it was me.

We make room to be loved completely when our hearts and minds are free to receive his acceptance.

See, rejection is funny. My expectation of acceptance was wrapped up in my own imagination. I had the story all written out in my head, and yet no one was following along with the "correct" script. When he rejected me, my little world came crashing down. All the time wasted, money stolen, rushed circles around the classroom, and the sheer devastation when I realized all he really liked were the cookies. He didn't like me. He liked the "me" that gave him cookies.

I was embarrassed, hurt, angry, and mostly defeated. I had pictured things ending (or beginning) much differently. But that's the problem when we picture in advance what can only be played out in the present. Sometimes we are wrong. Sometimes we are disappointed. Sometimes we are rejected.

Rejection hurts whether you're twelve or forty-two or ninety-two. Since that sixth-grade rejection, I wish I could say I have never felt those agonizing pangs again, but life doesn't always handle us with such care. There have been plenty of opportunities to learn how to deal with rejection. But, even greater than those lessons, have been the opportunities to see and know how God cares for me during the low moments of life. I am a walking billboard for the beauty of his goodness amid turmoil. I have faced rejection, infertility, job chaos, and much more. Just like you, sometimes those situations have been with grace, while at other times I've writhed under the weight of uncomfortable and disappointing circumstances.

What do we gain from rejection? I have experienced the enveloping arms of God, the ability to wipe away tears, and the capacity to breathe in a dose of hope.

That sixth-grade boy didn't have any idea I would document about our silly un-love story thirty-five years later. I have moved on down the road and found a guy who loves me and my chocolate chip cookies! It's a wonderful feeling to be accepted and loved. That's just what Jesus offers when we place our hurts and rejection at his feet. We make room to be loved completely when our hearts and minds are free to receive his acceptance.

Jesus is familiar with our pain. He says, "Follow me." That's our roadmap for dealing with the things that hurt the most. Follow Jesus—eyes filled with tears, fixed on him.

Stop and Reclaim

He came to his own, but his own people did not receive him. (John 1:11)

My God, my God, why have you forsaken me? (Matthew 27:46)

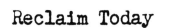

Reclaim Today

Journal your past hurt from rejection. How can the hurt bring you closer to God?

_____

_____

_____

_____

_____

_____

_____

_____

_____

_____

Sky High

Usually we don't purposefully put ourselves in positions where we need to be rescued. Sometimes, life just happens, and all of a sudden we find ourselves knee-deep (or sky high) in a situation where we have no control. Then we need help to get ourselves out of a mess.

Such was the case when I was thirteen years old. My church had sponsored a group trip to Six Flags over Georgia, a well-known amusement park nearby. I was excited to be going with friends. I'd saved my babysitting money to purchase my ticket, and I was sure this would be the best day of my life.

After hours of riding rollercoasters and water rides, it was almost time for my group to meet for the ride home. The rest of the group was on the opposite side of the park, so my friend and I jumped on the sky lift. I had ridden on a sky lift before, so there was no fear, no anxiousness, no nerves. As tired as we were, we looked forward to being able to sit down and rest our feet for a few minutes. Before my friend and I jumped into our seat on the sky lift, I noticed the sign said, "Just 15 minutes to the east entrance. Enjoy the ride." So we settled in for a few minutes of relaxation.

Five minutes into the ride, I felt the first sprinkle fall from the sky. Then another and another. Before long we were smack dab in the middle of a summer storm. Dangling in midair, my friend and I began to get nervous. The stress maximized when out of nowhere thunder rumbled. All of the sudden we lost power, and the sky lift stopped. We hung there, halfway across the park, sky high, soaking wet, and scared. Fear permeated the atmosphere. The darkness around us felt like it was closing in as power was out across the park. I whimpered. My friend cried. I could hear people yelling behind us in the next sky lift chair.

> We do not have to live in fear of the storm when we are held in the arms of God.

In less than ten minutes, what seemed like hours of waiting and utter terror, was over. The lights came back on all over the park, and our chair started moving. We had been rescued. Someone was working the whole time to rescue us.

The power outage wasn't my fault. I didn't place myself in a situation where I thought I would need rescuing. In fact, I had confidence and was fearless when I first sat down. I had no idea what the future would hold.

Friend, that's how it is when we walk with Jesus. Sometimes the circumstances impact us. We don't intend to get caught up in someone else's drama. We didn't ask for our spouse to cheat. We didn't plan to be in this financial situation. We prepare, but a thunderstorm comes out of nowhere and knocks out our power, leaving us stranded in darkness. In uncertain and fearful times, we can trust in a God who already has everything figured out. He has a plan and a purpose for our out-of-control situations.

Those uncertain times give us opportunities to trust that help is on the way. God doesn't abandon us. He goes through the storm with us. We are not always rescued from the suffering. We do not always receive earthly deliverance. However, we can experience the presence of God, sheltering us in place, providing peace and comfort. We do not have to live in fear of the storm when we are held in the arms of God.

Stop and Reclaim

God is our refuge and strength, a very present help in trouble. Therefore we will not fear though the earth gives way, though the mountains be moved into the heart of the sea. (Psalm 46:1–2)

Reclaim Today

What fear is holding you back from trusting God completely in the storm?

_____

_____

_____

_____

_____

_____

_____

_____

_____

_____

Confessions of a Liar

They say confession is good for the soul. And this is one time when they are right. Guilt can paralyze those who want to walk in freedom with the Lord.

I remember the first time I was old enough to understand that my sin had impacted the life of someone else. At nine years old, I knowingly used my words to hurt a friend. I had said something that was untrue, something that would make me look cool and worldly in front of my other so-called friends. I thought I could get away with it—that no one would know I was the culprit.

But it didn't go as I had planned. I got caught. Someone told my friend what I had said. She was hurt. Her parents were upset. I was embarrassed and terrified.

That night, the phone rang and I recognized the voice on the other end of the line. My friend's mom wanted to speak to my mom. Reluctantly, I handed the phone over. My heart was racing. I knew the next days of my life would be filled with punishments.

This, by far, was the worst sin I had ever committed in my life. I felt like I was the worst person who had walked the earth.

I heard the phone click and knew it would be just a matter of moments before my mom questioned me. My guilt was overwhelming. My heart raced. There she was, walking through the doorway of my bedroom. She paused and closed the door behind her. Then she made her way over to my bed, where I sat.

I started crying, sobbing really. My mom just sat there. Not a word came from her mouth until after I confessed it all. I told her what I had done. I confessed my lies and my hurtful behavior, and I told her how sorry I was for all I had done to my friend. I wept with remorse. My sin was right smack dab out there for her to see.

> *Paralyzing guilt can be transformed into life-giving freedom when we walk in the freedom of a life redeemed.*

And then she did the unexpected. My mom hugged me and told me she loved me. She said I needed to apologize and make things right with my friend and her family. Her countenance told me she was saddened by my choice. I would face the consequences of grounding along with the inevitable friendship loss.

I deserved everything I received. I went to school the next day, so anxious to see my friend. I was disappointed when my apology wasn't accepted with the same sweetness and forgiveness as my mom's response. That evening I called her mother to make things right, to admit my guilt and to ask for forgiveness. Her kindness overwhelmed me. A few days later, my friend and I were speaking again.

Guilt had weighed me down. The sin I had committed wrapped me in a web of deceit and fear. But love won. Just like Jesus does for us, my mom's response to my remorseful confession brought healing to my soul. When we come to Jesus full of brokenness for our sin, he reclaims those broken places although there may be restitution or consequences for our sin, we are forgiven. Paralyzing guilt can be transformed into life-giving freedom when we walk in the freedom of a life redeemed.

Stop and Reclaim

As it is, I rejoice, not because you were grieved, but because you were grieved into repenting. For you felt a godly grief, so that you suffered no loss through us. (2 Corinthians 7:9)

I confess my iniquity; I am sorry for my sin. (Psalm 38:18)

Reclaim Today

Is there a relationship in your life that needs healing and forgiveness. How can you move closer to reconciling with your friend?

_____

_____

_____

_____

_____

_____

_____

_____

_____

_____

_____

Bonus Dad

*G*ood fathers are rare. Sure, there are plenty of men who have "fathered" children but claiming the responsibility of raising a child is difficult. According to fatherhood.org, currently in the United States, 19.7 million children live in a home without a father. With numbers like that, we can agree that far too many fathers are not following through on their responsibilities. I am very blessed to have had a father who stayed, loved my mother fiercely, and loved his three children unconditionally.

And then my father died. He was just forty-five, and our family was left with a gaping hole at the head of the table. Those first few years without him were numbing as my mom did her best to finish raising three teenagers while she herself grieved the love of her youth.

For nearly twenty years, we muddled through Father's Days, his birthday, and the anniversaries that should have been celebrated. We each grieved in our own ways. His children were married, his grandbabies were born. Life went on.

And then (at least for me) God relieved us, filling that emptiness with a bonus dad. My mom met an incredible man and fell head over heels for him. For the last ten years I have found room in my heart for another father.

I am sharing this, because we all desire a father figure in our lives, even if we don't realize it. I never knew I wanted another dad—until I had the opportunity to have one. And now, for these last few years, a beautiful love has developed between Pop and me.

Loving Pop doesn't mean I love my dad less.

Loving Pop doesn't mean I don't miss my dad.

Loving Pop doesn't mean that I abandon memories and special times with my dad.

It does mean that I can embrace full-heartedly the provision God has given me for an earthly father figure. I have room in my heart to love him. I have a need in my life for his counsel and wisdom. It's my choice to let him have space in my life—and I choose it!

I also have the distinct joy of watching him be a grandpa to my kids, a loving husband to my mother, and a provider of stable and strong leadership every family needs. It's a win-win for me.

> God's way of redeeming and reclaiming can mean we have to let go of what we think things should look like.

The blessing of his friendship far outweighs the risk of losing anything.

At a most vulnerable time in my family's life a few years ago, Pop showed up on my doorstep with my mom. He's a man of few words, and most of those happen behind a fishing pole or a hunting rifle. He didn't offer any profound wisdom; he didn't try to fix anything (except the exhaust fan in the bathroom), and he didn't tell us everything would be OK. Nope. He just showed up, loved on us, and did what millions of "fathers" don't do. He stayed for as long as we needed him. He stayed spiritually and prayerfully, ready to do whatever was needed. That's a good father.

In 2019, after our house flooded from Tropical Storm Imelda, Pop showed up again with tools in hand, a truck full of bleach, plenty of garbage bags, and a huge hug for each of us. For over a week, he worked ten to twelve hours each day. He helped rip out walls and box up the things we could salvage. When it was time to go, he prayed a blessing over us and our ruined home. This is what real fathers do.

The Bible says, "He who finds a wife finds a good thing" (Proverbs 18:22). I'm pretty sure we were on the benefiting end of Pop finding a wife. In my book, the family who finds a bonus dad like Pop finds a good thing!

Sometimes in life we don't always understand or know what we need. That's not our job anyway. God knows what we need. And, in his time, he supplies everything. As an adult daughter of a bonus dad, my heart could have stayed closed when he came on the scene. I could have shut him out, rejected his love, even questioned his motives. It would have been easy to say, "I already had a dad, and I don't need a replacement." But I would have missed so much. I would have been the loser.

God's way of redeeming and reclaiming can mean we have to let go of what we think things should look like. Do I trust God to reclaim and repurpose my ideas with the big picture of his perfect will? His vision for me is perfect. It's 20/20.

Stop and Reclaim

This God—his way is perfect; the word of the LORD proves true; he is a shield for all those who take refuge in him. (Psalm 18:30)

Reclaim Today

Is there a relationship that God has given you that was unexpected? What have you gained? How can you give thanks to God for this provision?

_____

_____

_____

_____

_____

_____

_____

_____

_____

_____

Gut-Punched

$\mathcal{I}$ was only sixteen years old when I knew God was calling me into the ministry. I wasn't exactly sure what he was asking of me, so I decided I would head to Bible college. Certainly the prospects of meeting a like-minded ministry man would be much higher there than anywhere else. I had hopes I would meet a man preparing to be a pastor. The idea of being a pastor's wife appealed to me.

I had been raised in the same church for the bulk of my childhood, under the same pastor and around the same beautiful congregation. Because of my naivety and innocence, I didn't know about the hazards and hardships of serving the Lord with your life. I didn't know that there would be magnificent days of "Praise the Lord!" and heartbreaking days of "Please let this cup pass from me."

At Bible college I did meet and marry that like-minded ministry man. Bruce and I had been in ministry only a short time before we experienced our first surprise betrayal. Quickly, my defenses shot up, and I started building a protective wall around our marriage and ministry. No one would hurt us that way again. I would make sure it never ever happened again.

But then it did. Words twisted. Mistakes magnified. Human efforts failed. Year after year, hurts and disappointments started building. Instead of feeling protected by my wall, I felt imprisoned by fear, bitterness, and anger. I was disappointed with God and frustrated with people. And I was tired—oh, so tired.

Bruce was beyond defeated. His morale was low, like an old dog kicked to the curb. The burden of the gospel weighed heavy on his shoulders. His heart struggled to keep going. Discouragement and disheartened sadness began to set in. I felt like his heart was aching and oozing for all to see. It was an awful time.

Until it wasn't. Within a few months' time, we resigned the church we had loved and served. Those people were like family, and many didn't understand why we were leaving. There were unanswered questions, even skeptics and gossips who wanted to be heard. There was chaos. It grieved us to watch people we loved hurting. And it hurt to be hurting too.

But God did not leave us there. Within weeks of stepping away from ministry, God began refueling and encouraging us. He used people in our community, friends from ministry, and our own families to breathe life into our tired bones. His Word was alive in us.

His days in the grave didn't change his heart for people.

Bible verses and stories fed and guided us. What had been drought and barren land was becoming fertile soil for God to plant his new vision for our lives. The future began unfolding.

It would require sacrifice, discomfort, willing spirits, and cooperation. But God was doing more than we could imagine, even amid the hurt and disappointments. He was reclaiming our hearts for ministry.

Maybe you've been hurt while serving others. Maybe you feel drained and used up, like you have nothing left to give. What I know about God is he doesn't leave us during those times of grief. He will heal your hurting heart; he will comfort your soul like no one else. He will care for you with compassion. With confidence I can say God can and will renew your heart for ministry. It may look different than before, but he is all about renewal.

When I look at Jesus's example of service, I see a Savior who died on the cross by the most brutal tactics. He was mocked and rejected, yet, just three days later, was back in the ministry saddle—serving, loving, and caring for the worst of sinners. Sinners just like me. His days in the grave didn't change his heart for people. Our days of hurt and feeling unappreciated, discouraged, and tired don't have to change our hearts either. We may need a moment, a month, or a change of pace, but God wants to renew and restore us.

Stop and Reclaim

For God is not unjust so as to overlook your work and the love that you have shown for his name in serving the saints, as you still do. (Hebrews 6:10)

Reclaim Today

How has the church ministered to you during times of hurt and heartache? Take time to thank the Lord for their ministry toward you.

_____

_____

_____

_____

_____

_____

_____

_____

_____

_____

_____

_____

Beautiful Messes

*B*eautiful melodies have started by playing and humming notes until those notes became phrases and phrases became songs. Those initial messes or missed notes and pitches didn't randomly happen. Someone worked with diligence and creativity to compose the perfect song. I'm curious to know how many beautiful mistakes Frank Sinatra or Elvis Presley or Dolly Parton made before getting their songs on the radio. I like to imagine that like me, they've made their share of mistakes.

Beautiful mistakes are made when we are in the throes of intentionally trying. We may be trying to write a new song, learn a new sport, or parent a two-year-old. These challenges encourage us to persevere, to keep trying, to stay the course. These mistakes are beautiful, because they reflect the human spirit. The go-get-er-done attitude. That persevering attitude is in the student, the parent, the author, the athlete. And sometimes . . . it's in me.

I don't really like messing up, but I know it's worth working through the mistakes. It's worth it to try hard and to persevere. In fact, it's completely biblical. We're told to keep on keepin' on, in James 1:2–4.

> Count it all joy, my brothers, when you meet trials of various kinds, for you know that the testing of your faith produces steadfastness. And let steadfastness have its full effect, that you may be perfect and complete, lacking in nothing.

God's job is to worry about the end result. Ours is to be faithful to the task that he's called us to do. And if, along the way, things get a little crazy—we hit some wrong notes or a foul ball or yell at the kids a time or two—just get back to the business you're called to do. We're not trying to earn anything by our trying. In fact, our mistakes prove we can't earn anything. It's in these mistakes we find we need God the most. Without him we can do nothing. When we struggle and put forth our best effort, God is watching. He sees our feeble attempts as we try to raise kids, work jobs, serve in church, and coach soccer. Better than that, sees our hearts. He sees our motives, and he sees our beautiful mistakes. Each and every one. He loves us enough to make us beautiful in his time.

God uses broken, handicapped people all the time.

Our imperfections show how badly we need him. As I sit here and type, I look at the Band-Aid covering an imperfection on my arm. Today I sat in the dermatologist's office while the doctor numbed my arm, removed a small growth, and used three stitches to patch my skin back together. Now I wait for a pathology report, which I trust will be fine. This imperfection, this blemish, this mistake (according to the world) has drawn me closer to Jesus. Closer to trusting him, closer to believing him, closer to wanting his will. That's what makes it beautiful. What he's doing in you makes your mistakes, your blemishes, your melody line less disastrous. It's grace.

So, don't give up! Persevering makes your messes beautiful. God's right there beside you putting the finishing touches on something better than you can imagine. He's drawing you closer to himself. Don't resist. He wants to make your mistakes beautiful too.

Think about what he did for these people:

- Rahab, prostitute turned ancestor to Jesus Christ
- Moses, stutterer turned leader of Israel
- Paul, persecutor of Christians turned evangelist for Christ

God uses broken, handicapped people all the time. He's ready for you. Persevere, my friend. When you stumble, trip, or hit a wrong note, stay close to him. You're his masterpiece, even in the midst of your mistakes.

Stop and Reclaim

Be watchful, stand firm in the faith, act like men, be strong. (1 Corinthians 16:13)

Reclaim Today

How is God using your mistakes to create something beautiful?

_____

_____

_____

_____

_____

_____

_____

_____

_____

_____

_____

_____

_____

Seventeen Seconds of Stay

Our huge Australian Shepherd, Maks, keeps things lively around our house. Between his infatuation with our calico cat and his fake starvation techniques, the dog keeps us hopping. Typically his breed enjoys the outdoors, but not Maks. He enjoys the high life of air conditioning, soft rugs, and lots of hands-on loving.

Not too long ago, my daughter decided to try some obedience training with Maks. Until then, Maks had been relegated to the sunroom, kitchen, and dining room area. This was largely due to his inability to hide his excitement when anyone new entered the house, which usually led to a quick, unwelcomed sprinkling of our guests. We had crate trained him and taught him to sit, but "stay" had been a challenge.

So, Savannah decided to work with him on strengthening his staying power. We took down the gate that had separated his territory from the rest of the house. Savannah told him to stay and then walked to the piano room at the front of the house. The first time,

Maks lasted seven seconds before we heard his paws tippy toe down the hallway. The second time, it was thirteen seconds. We were so proud of him. And the third time, at seventeen seconds, he was so reluctant to disobey. He peeked around the corner, made eye contact with me, and knew he was guilty! Seventeen seconds. That's it! That's all the dear pup could muster–just seventeen seconds of loyal obedience.

> He peeked around the corner, made eye contact with me, and knew he was guilty!

Before I could stop shaking my head, I thought of how I am so often the same way. I can walk in obedience for about seventeen seconds, and then God must shake his head at me and wonder what in the world I am doing. Seventeen seconds of being loyal to the one who cared enough to die on a cross for me. Seventeen seconds of unabandoned fear and timidity. Seventeen seconds of God powered bravery—completely free to obey. And yet, I throw away opportunities to live in obedience all the time.

And then I get distracted, much like my dog. Something comes my way that makes me feel better, more fulfilled, or more important. Seventeen seconds, more or less, is all any of us obey, because we're never completely obedient. Not obeying is disobeying, and we are all experts on that.

God is full of grace and patience. He knows my heart, and how I want to be obedient and loyal. How often I've become like Jonah or the children of Israel who also had trouble getting passed those seventeen seconds of obedience. In like fashion, he corrects me, sets me back on the right track, and loves me unconditionally, just like he does for all his children. He offers me freedom and protection in the circle of obedience. Why would I want to live any other way?

So when you find yourself at the seventeen second mark, press on. The test is worth passing! And when you fail, know that with arms wide open, God wants you back. In a heartbeat, he says, "Try, try again." With his strength you can do better!

Stop and Reclaim

If you know these things, blessed are you if you do them. (John 13:17)

Reclaim Today

What is an area where you struggle to obey God? How can you set yourself up for better success?

_____

_____

_____

_____

_____

_____

_____

_____

_____

_____

_____

_____

Sunday Defense

For years my husband and I have had a Sunday plan for success. It goes a little something like this: he leaves the house before anyone else wakes up, and the rest of the family goes to church in a separate vehicle. We do this, because we were victims of an attack early in our married life.

We were totally unprepared for the attack. I had never heard anyone ever talk of the attack before. It had never crossed my mind that we would be prime candidates for such a vicious and hurtful fight. Little did we know that inch by inch we would innocently allow the predator to sneak in and plant little bombs that would go off in our home.

The first ten years of our marriage, we were childless. We were carefree and flying high. On weekends, we could stay up late, watch movies, go to the store at midnight, eat ice cream for break-fast. There was little recourse for our unwise decisions. And then we had kids.

Sunday mornings became a bit more laborious. They required careful and skillful planning to maneuver successfully. Before the first attack things had run smoothly. I took care of myself; Bruce took care of himself. Then there were two other little lives crying for our attention. Getting out of the house became a crazy game of hide-and-seek—hide from the spit up and seek refuge in coffee and Diet Coke.

The attacks became more aggressive. Tensions would run high as we fought with each other over things like packing the diaper bag, changing the diapers one more time, and suctioning snotty noses. Inevitably smaller surprise attacks would occur, and suddenly hairbows, bow ties and shoelaces were candidates for full-blown arguments.

And that's when I realized the enemy had been working hard to get us to fall into the Sunday morning trap. The one where the parents look like they've been frazzled by the warzone tactics. Only this was spiritual warfare. So, we decided to start preparing on Saturday night for the Sunday-morning war. We packed the diaper bag, laid out clothes, and showered in the evening. We went to bed earlier and stopped the midnight runs for ice cream. Saturdays meant eating at home instead of going out. All this preparation so that Sunday mornings wouldn't look like something out of a G. I. Joe Magazine.

And we started winning. Not every time, but most of the time. When we finally realized that we weren't warring against each other, when we realized that Satan had a very definite plan to get under our skin on Sunday mornings, when we started paying attention to his tactics—we started winning.

The same can be true in every area of our lives: school mornings, business meetings, dealing with our in-laws, or a neighborhood misunderstanding. Satan sets little traps of frustration, anger, or miscommunication, so that you fall into them and feel defeated, discouraged, and ready to quit. Don't fall for his tricks. His schemes are easily identifiable, if we are paying attention. When we realize we aren't fighting against each other but against an enemy of dark forces, we can make and work a plan that will defeat him. He's no match for our God.

Reclaim your days for the Lord. Don't let the enemy take one more moment from you. Be alert. Make a plan. Strategize with others about how they defeat the enemy. Do things that are within your control. Don't allow Satan to have unlimited resources of your family, time, money, and talents. For example, if you're on a diet, don't keep a hidden stash of your favorite candy bars in the house. Save yourself the heartache of day-one defeat by chucking the sugar drinks before your "drink more water" thirty-day challenge begins. You see, we can help ourselves.

> Decide today that you are on the side of victory.

Use Scripture to defeat the enemy whenever you can. Satan's best and most cherished title is "Father of Lies." A clear way to defeat him is in representing truth as a habit in our lives. Read the words of truth (the Bible). Memorize the truths of God's Word, meditate on the truths of the Way, the Truth, and the Life (Jesus). The enemy will not be able to dig his heels in where truth is prevalent. He hates the truth. Decide today that you are on the side of victory.

Stop and Reclaim

Be sober-minded; be watchful. Your adversary the devil prowls around like a roaring lion, seeking someone to devour. (1 Peter 5:8)

Every word of God proves true; he is a shield to those who take refuge in him. (Proverbs 30:5)

Reclaim Today

Do you feel the attack of the enemy on a certain area of your life? If so, create a plan of action to fight against him.

_____

_____

_____

_____

_____

_____

_____

_____

_____

Tearless Yesterdays

I didn't cry in public for a long time. Mistakenly, somewhere along the way of life, my tears became a sign of weakness. Or at least that's what I thought and felt. So I would cry, but it would be in private, at home or in the car or with my husband—never with others. It was too revealing, too transparent for my liking.

And so, through the years, I became hardened. I could sit with someone who was going through terrible loss and remain emotionless. Some viewed it as a strength and commented, "I don't know how you can be so strong at a time like this."

But the truth is, what some saw as strength, I knew was actually weakness—an inability to let others close, an avoidance of reality, a quenching of the Holy Spirit, a mercy-less spirit. I lacked compassion, empathy and a heart that would weep with those who weep. I was shallow and although I was friendly with others, I had no one close enough to call a good friend.

Then, one day, my hurts were more than I could manage

stuffing into my heart, and I finally burst into tears over things that crushed my spirit. I cried for almost two days straight. As I cried, I reviewed those moments that had torn my heart apart. I reclaimed the moments of loss and sadness that I had tucked away.

There I sat, right smack dab in the middle of those moments, and I grieved the losses, the sadness, the death, the hurt. I acknowledged my part in moments of sin. I let words of hurt and disappointment cover the pages of journals and make their way to the ears of God. Tears washed over me like a shower of blessings. The flood of tears cleaned the cobwebs of bitterness and anger; they rinsed away sorrow and the sadness I had brought on myself.

Those tears were part of the most refreshing and cleansing relief I had ever experienced. If you've ever known the benefit of a "good" cry, then you know what I am talking about.

> I found peace and comfort in letting go of the need to control those ugly circumstances.

Reclaiming my tears didn't leave me in a state of sadness. It provided relief, like a dam breaking under the pressure of the weighty water. I found peace and comfort in letting go of the need to control those ugly circumstances. I found refuge in a Savior who can handle my feelings, tears, and fears. I found friendship in weeping with others during hard times and rejoicing with them in the good times.

God made a way for us to express ourselves through our emotions. What might seem like weakness can be used to strengthen not just your faith but the faith of those around you. People don't need to see a super human who never has troubles or always experiences success. The world needs to see compassionate, kind and empathetic Christians who have experienced real world problems and struggles and have found their answers in Christ.

Stand in the truth that God made our tears as well as our smiles. He can use both to reclaim our days.

Stop and Reclaim

The LORD is a stronghold for the oppressed, a stronghold in times of trouble. (Psalm 9:9)

Hear my prayer, O LORD; let my cry come to you! Do not hide your face from me in the day of my distress! Incline your ear to me; answer me speedily in the day when I call! (Psalm 102:1–2)

Reclaim Today

Make a list of emotions and scripture connections. God gave us these emotions to express ourselves in appropriate ways. Can you recall a time someone else's emotional response helped you deal with something you were feeling?

_____

_____

_____

_____

_____

_____

_____

_____

_____

_____

_____

I Hate Who I Am

My sandwich and onion rings lay uneaten on the red Dairy Queen tray. I sipped my Diet Coke occasionally but mostly just listened as a broken woman told me her broken story of abuse, abandonment, fear, cigarettes, poverty, and other issues I had only heard about. They were issues I had feared and prayed against. Then she said the words, "I hate who I am."

Hate. Such a small word with such big meaning. The dictionary definition is "to feel extreme enmity toward: to have a strong aversion to: find very distasteful, to express or feel extreme enmity or active hostility."[1]

"I hate who I am." I thought about correcting her. I thought about explaining to her that she shouldn't hate what God had beautifully fashioned. I thought about telling her how much there was to love about herself. But I think I must have heard God whisper, "She hates herself because she doesn't know me. She hates

1 Merriam-Webster, s.v. "Hate," accessed September 3, 2020, https://www.merri-am-webster.com/dictionary/hate/.

what the enemy has done to her life. She hates who she has become because of sin."

And very suddenly I felt the ground leveling between us. How many times have I hated myself when I have allowed distance to come between the Father and me? How many times have I hated myself when I have allowed the devil to win a victory in my life? How many times have I hated myself when sin has uglied my life with lies, insecurity, and doubts? And there, in one moment,

> ... she felt the warfare around her ...

through the tears falling from my eyes, I saw my own reflection.

But there's a difference. A big, essential difference. I know about the antidote for self-hatred. In my soul, I know there is something that defeats those feelings and emotions of complete failure and self-loathing. I've experienced that washing away of guilt, worthlessness, and humiliation. Peace and joy have been my companions because of one thing.

Grace.

Grace doesn't keep track of my failures, my past, my choices, my bad decisions. Grace comes in and washes away my hate. Grace quietly springs up like hope and blessing in my life. And, as if there could be nothing more amazing, I am reminded I have not done one single thing to deserve that grace.

The broken woman and I sat and talked until well past our meals growing cold. She grabbed my hand and nearly . . . almost . . . reached out for Jesus. It was as if she felt the warfare around her, the slight breeze of an angel's sword as it lashed out and grazed the face of a demon. The warfare was every bit spiritual. The battle for her soul was so very real. But then she said, "I need to wait. I need to think on these things . . . "My heart sank. Not because I need to be there when she begins this walk of love, but because I knew. I've been there. I've felt the breeze . . .

The reclaimed know the urgency of the battle. They've lived through it. In desperation, in addiction, in self-hatred, the urgency can be tainted by the belief that things will get better on their own. Self-hatred is a snare, a trick. The lies of the enemy are easily believed in the hearts of the defeated. And we've all been defeated. We all must remember that there is still a battle to be won. There is still an enemy to fight.

Stop and Reclaim

For we do not wrestle against flesh and blood, but against the rulers, against the authorities, against the cosmic powers over this present darkness, against the spiritual forces of evil in heavenly places. (Ephesians 6:12)

Do not be deceived: neither the sexually immoral, nor idolaters, nor adulterers, nor men who practice homosexuality, no thieves, nor the greedy, nor drunkards, nor revilers, nor swindlers will inherit the kingdom of God. And such were some of you. But you were washed, you were sanctified, you were justified in the name of the Lord Jesus Christ and by the Spirit of our God. (1 Corinthians 6:9–11)

Reclaim Today

What is an area that you feel spiritually attacked? How can you develop a better plan so you do not succumb to the attacks?

_____

_____

_____

_____

_____

_____

_____

_____

_____

_____

_____

Hurt and Healing

*T*he worst hurt I've experienced has been through the local church. As a pastor's wife, I can also say the best moments of my life, outside of the births of my children, have been through the local church. The body of Christ has both hurt me and, through Christ, has healed me.

God's design for the local church is to function as a body—a living, breathing body—full of life, energy, power, and vision. He has designed that body like ours, with specific parts and purposes. Each body part operates in submission to the head (Christ) and works hard to be efficient and productive. But there is no perfect body.

It's interesting to see how each local body of Christ functions. I have been in churches where the body has a big mouth. Their voice seems to be their primary body part; rarely is this a good thing. I have been in other churches where their hands were the main functioning part of the body. They worked and served. Still other churches had huge feet; through their pocketbooks and presence, they were consumed with spreading the gospel. In another church I sensed a healthy heart where the people, though small in number, had a huge heart for ministry and the gospel.

The truth is that one functioning part in the body doesn't mean the body is strong. The dysfunctional parts of the body can spread disease, infection, and general bad health. It's a depressing scenario.

Through years of ministry, I have learned that God, who desires a bride/groom relationship with the church, is the head. He's where the brain is, where vision and hearing originate. We are just mere parts who should be guided by a perfect, all-knowing God. As a church member, a pastor's wife, a choir member, a Vacation Bible School worker or a Sunday School teacher, my job is to examine the gifts God has given me and use my spiritual muscle to develop a body that is spiritually fit, healthy, and in-tune with the rest of the body parts. Working together, we accomplish more than if we are constantly in chaos, fighting each other.

When we are hurt, angry, or frustrated, it's easy to want to quit: quit listening, quit encouraging, quit serving, quit ministry. Quit all together. You get the picture. And I've been there. The diseased parts of the body have a way of infecting other parts of the body until what was once just a small sore becomes an infectious disease, ravaging the entire body.

God is the antibody we all need. He has the power to cure the diseases of the church: the laziness and selfishness, the gossip and slander, the pride and abuse. He is the head. He has the power to control the entire body with one thought, one word, one motion. So why doesn't he?

I believe it has to do with our free will. Our choice to do his will (and not ours) is an act of love, submission, and humility. When the body of Christ is functioning in the spirit of love, submission, and humility toward the Lord and others, we will see a healthier body.

That's the kind of body that helps heal the broken. That's the kind of body that takes a broken pastor's wife of twenty-five years and loves her. It genuinely embraces her, extends more kindness than she could possibly deserve, and showers her with affirming words. As I read over those words it might seem as if I think I deserve these things. And now, after some time in a healthier body, I realize I do. We all do. We all deserve to be loved fully, embraced in sincerity, shown kindness, and given respect—not because of a title or a name, but because that's how the body of Christ should function.

I've been disease-free for a few years now. And I am happy to say the diseased body that hurt me so badly is getting healthier. What have I learned? Focus on the head of the body. He is the only part of the body that is free of the sin and grime of this world. He will not fail. I've also learned that sometimes we need a transplant. Sometimes it's the right thing to do. To be transplanted into a new body might hurt a little and take some adjusting. You might need to take it easy for a little bit, before you dive in to all the things. But soon . . . soon, you'll be acclimated and ready to fully commit to help this new body function in a healthy manner.

And sometimes God says stay. Stay and fight the disease. Fight it like chemotherapy to cancer. It will be hard. It will be painful. Most days you will want to give up. But your faithfulness will be rewarded. Your confidence in God, your head, will sustain you. And your love for his church will allow others to be strengthened.

Only God knows what is right for you. His church needs to be reclaimed—not because he has disowned it, but because we have. What the world sees is a distorted body—at best, a diseased body, and at worst, a corpse. There's nothing appealing about either.

Let's be the generation who, with Christ as the head, brings back the healthy church.

Stop and Reclaim

And I tell you, you are Peter, and on this rock I will build my church, and the gates of hell shall not prevail against it. (Matthew 16:18)

And let us consider how we may stir up one another to love and good works, not neglecting to meet together, as is the habit of some, but encouraging one another, and all the more as you see the Day drawing near. (Hebrews 10:24–25)

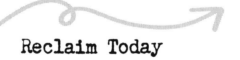

Reclaim Today

How can you help reclaim your church for Christ? Are you part of the healing or the disease? Consider how you can stir up love in the body of Christ.

_____

_____

_____

_____

Eleven Years and Counting

*E*leven years ago, I met Jaime and Felicia. We all drove minivans and were affectionately called the Minivan Mafia. Between the three of us we have ten kids, who were between the ages of three and ten years of age at that time; one more was born shortly after we met. We were moms in the throes of motherhood, knee-deep in laundry, snotty noses, bad hairstyles, and caffeine addiction.

We met through church, but our relationship really took off after we took a Bible study together. We would go to Bible study, pen and notebooks in hand. Afterward, we'd rehash it on the way home. We were real scholars, asking the tough questions, trying to grow in faith.

Actually, who am I kidding? We were in survival mode. We were thankful for the two hours with other adults who weren't begging us to color, play, or read to them. And we were in it for the occasional after-the-Bible-study-Whataburger meal. Don't get me wrong. We loved our families deeply. It was out of love for them, and our sanity, that we attended Bible study together.

Through the years we broke bread and studied the Bible together many times. We grew as our kids did. We said hard things to each other as our trust deepened. And we loved each other as our hearts grew in love for one another.

You can say you love each other and never know the depth until one of you gets called to the mission field. We knew it was coming. When our church invited missionaries to present their mission projects, the look in Jaime's eyes gave it away. Her husband, a commercial pilot, had talked for years about flying planes filled with Bibles to people groups who had never had the Word of God in their native language. We knew she would be leaving us. We knew her heart would live in two places, but her body would be moving 10,000 miles away.

> We were moms in the throes of motherhood, knee-deep in laundry, snotty noses, bad hairstyles, and caffeine addiction.

It happened. And other things happened. Our kids started growing up, so there were first loves, drivers' licenses, and college. We cared for pets, parents, and grandparents. We tackled returning to the workforce, navigated the ups and downs of ministry, and shared a few more Whataburger meals.

And then I moved away. In a tangled web of events, what I thought would never happen, happened. Even though five hours isn't that far, it's far enough. At a time in life when I needed my friends close, God chose to move us. And I reluctantly obeyed.

Friendship has never been easy for me. I'm sure it's not easy for people trying to befriend me either. I am a weird combo of extrovert and introvert; sometimes I need people, and sometimes I don't. But I really needed these people. They had been my sisters, my confidants, my warriors in prayer. How could I make it without either of them?

And now, two years later, we have survived. With the help of the Good Lord and modern technology, we have kept close. We text and call. Sometimes, Felicia and I get together to exchange kids for a weekend or when one of us needs a listening ear. God didn't forsake me. He may have changed our course, but the destination is the same. Felicia is a church secretary now, Jaime a missionary, and I'm still a pastor's wife. We could run a small country with all we know. Whenever Jaime is in the U.S., we always make time to visit—usually at Whataburger.

God has brought us through rough times with each other, misunderstandings, grief, anger and much more . . . and all those things make me love each of these women even more.

Friendship for women can be hard. It takes time, effort, and patience. For us, there are weddings, colleges, and menopause in our future. We will grieve for one another as we bury our remaining parents. We will share lots of photos when we become grandmothers. We will be present even though thousands of miles separate us. The future is bright, because I have the faithfulness of a couple of true friends.

That relationship you miss? The friend you want to be? Reclaim it today. Grab hold of the good stuff that comes from growing together, and hang on for the ride! It's going to be great!

Stop and Reclaim

Oil and perfume make the heart glad, and the sweetness of a friend comes from his earnest counsel. (Proverbs 27:9)

Beloved, if God so loved us, we also ought to love one another. (1 John 4:11)

Reclaim Today

Make a list of your top friends and invite them over. Share a glass of sweet tea and remind them why you love them so much.

_____

_____

_____

_____

_____

_____

_____

_____

_____

Wasted Moments

I sat in the chair, staring into space. I had been there for over an hour. Numbed by the pain of disappointment, worry, and fear, I could not move. It wasn't the first time it had happened. No, I had become a pro at wasting valuable moments, because I was paralyzed by circumstances. This time it was money, but the last time it was hurt feelings. The time before that, it was over someone else's angry words. It seemed more and more often I was wasting minutes replaying the difficult things happening in my life.

Maybe it's happened to you. Marriage problems, financial woes, rebellious children, an illness—any of those things can cause a pause in our lives. It's not unusual for people to miss work, church, or family obligations due to dealing with the pressures of life. Sometimes the calendar shuts down altogether to make room for our grief and disappointment. And sometimes that is OK.

But for me, as I sat paralyzed for the third time in not too many days, I realized I wasn't spending time doing positive things:

praying, thinking of solutions, or counting my blessings. No, I was rehashing every painful moment. Over and over and over. It was ugly. It was depressing. It was beating me down.

A few days later, I was scrolling through Pinterest and found a quote that said, "Have you prayed about it as much as you've complained about it?" I thought about that for a minute. I had sure worried, replayed, yelled internally at myself, and blamed others for my problems. But I thought I had been too angry to pray. So, I hadn't prayed about it at all.

I was angry. I was disappointed. I was worried. But wasting moments wasn't solving

> Wasted moments turn quickly into wasted hours. Wasted hours turn into wasted days. And wasted days turn into a wasted life.

any of my problems. Wasted moments turn quickly into wasted hours. Wasted hours turn into wasted days. And wasted days turn into a wasted life. When I am honest and real with myself, I know that's not the life I want.

So I prayed.

Now, mind you, it wasn't the orderly sort of prayer you hear at church on Sunday morning. It was more of a confusion of tearful words thrown down at the feet of Jesus with the hope that in his intercession for me to God the Father, he might be able to make some sort of sense of all the mumbo jumbo. It was honest, raw, and included words like, "I was stupid . . . they were jerks . . . please forgive me . . . I don't like the way I feel." I'm sure Jesus handled the chaotic babble just fine.

In the process of learning, I am discovering the weight of my worry and disappointments is too heavy for me to bear. It's overwhelming. I am too weak to carry it. While we learn from our mistakes, we are not meant to carry around a scrapbook filled with daily reminders of our mess ups. In fact, God says he buries our sin as far as the east is from the west (Psalm 103:12.) He used a measure that we would understand to remind us that our mistakes and sins have been taken care of. We don't need to dig it up, wear it, think about it, worry about it, share it or do it any longer. He has dealt with it, and it is finished.

The days of wasting hours worrying over different outcomes, what-ifs, has-beens and what-might-have-beens are over. I won't say that I don't fall into the trap of a moment or two, here and there. But the reclaiming of my days is faster now that I know and understand that praying, forgiveness and moving on are divine options God has given me to have peace and comfort.

Reclaim your moments today. Don't stay in bondage. Focus on the things God has planned for your day and move toward those goals. The enemy will be defeated as we walk in the freedom of our next moments with Christ.

Stop and Reclaim

For freedom Christ has set us free; stand firm therefore, and do not submit again to a yoke of slavery. (Galatians 5:1)

Reclaim Today

What are you wasting your time worrying about?

_____

_____

_____

_____

_____

_____

_____

_____

_____

_____

_____

_____

_____

The Potter

About fourteen years ago, my family began visiting Gatlinburg, Tennessee, for vacation. The Smoky Mountains, slow pace, and gorgeous sunsets were factors in making this a place we have repeatedly visited. We enjoy the local attractions, including the local southern food and the craftsmen's loop in Gatlinburg.

Known as the Great Smoky Arts and Crafts Community, it's full of artisans who paint, weave, sew, build, cook, pour candles, woodwork, carve, forge, and (our favorite) throw pottery. After years of touring, we found our family favorite, a potter at Alewine Pottery.

We enjoy watching Alewine family members throw, dry, glaze and fire pottery. The process is long, tedious, detailed, and beautiful. Each step is carefully completed with the gentle hands of the potter. Each piece of pottery is created with the buyer in mind, delicately designed by the one who knows the clay the best. The potter knows the exact amount of water required to form that particular piece, the pressure needed to carve the design, the right amount of glaze to make it shine, and the amount of heat necessary to make it a vessel that will last for generations. This is no light task. The usefulness of the pottery is only as good as the skill of the potter.

The Bible tells us God is our potter (Isaiah 64:8.) We are the clay in his hands, to become what he wants us to be. It can be painful as he kneads the clay to remove impurities. We may look like a mess before we look like masterpieces. Sometimes you just have to get a "God's eye view" to see that the Master Potter is scooping up all the rubble and ruin from your low places to mold and create good in your life. His love reaches down into the dirt, out of what you may think is utter defeat or hopelessness. Then he lifts you up from what you may view as worthless into something truly worthwhile.

> The usefulness of the pottery is only as good as the skill of the potter.

The process is beautiful to watch from the window at Alewine Pottery. I can imagine what it looks like from God's viewpoint as he molds and makes us into his masterpieces. However painful it is for me, the end result is a beautiful, useful vessel. As the Master Potter reshapes and reforms the wet clay, I may not understand what he is doing, but I don't have to worry in his hands. It would only be scary if I didn't trust the hands of the Potter.

For many years I have questioned the specific purpose of my life. Many of our purposes are outlined directly in the Bible: an obedient daughter, a loving wife, a wise mother, a godly woman.

But what about the day-to-day: career, friends, dreams, goals, and plans? The lessons in the process of reclaiming every day have taught me that when I am moldable, pliable and submit to the Potter, he will give me purpose for that day. It might be loving my neighbor, taking dinner to a friend, or listening to my child talk about a hard day at school.

For some reason, along the way, I lost sense of real purpose. Maybe it was when my stinkin' thinkin' believed that God somehow categorizes us by titles. Mother, wife, and teacher seem like small titles up against CEO, business owner, pastor, or doctor. But God sees the obedience of the heart. Plain and simple obedience— not the size of a job or a big title. What a fantastic way to reclaim our purpose! When I understand there are no small jobs with the Lord, no small purposes, no worthless tasks I become a usable vessel in God's collection of pottery.

Stop and Reclaim

But now, O Lord, you are our Father; we are the clay, and you are our potter; we are all the work of your hand. (Isaiah 64:8)

Now in a great house there are not only vessels of gold and silver but also of wood and clay, some for honorable use, some for dishonorable. Therefore, if anyone cleanses himself from what is dishonorable, he will be a vessel for honorable use, set apart as holy, useful to the master of the house, ready for every good work. (2 Timothy 2:20–21)

But we have this treasure in jars of clay, to show that the surpassing power belongs to God and not to us. (2 Corinthians 4:7)

Reclaim Today

Are you willing to be shaped by the Master? What areas need remaking most?

_____

_____

_____

_____

_____

_____

_____

_____

_____

Three New Dresses

$\mathcal{M}$y dad worked at a department store for most of my child-hood. He was paid a decent salary and small commission on whatever he sold and received a good discount for anything he bought at the store. We were not rich, but I didn't know if we were poor or not for most of my childhood. Looking back now, I know. I understand better the way my mom cooked, like the breakfast-for-dinner trick and the stew-the-day-after-roast event. I remember the garden, the hand-me-downs, and an un-written commandment that did not allow for the air conditioner to be turned on until after 3:00 p.m. during the summertime. I get it. We were the middle class of DeKalb County, Georgia. Not poor. Not rich.

New clothes were a luxury. I remember a lot of secondhand shopping, the neighbor girl's hand-me-downs, and homemade clothes. I do not remember receiving new clothes very often. But on one special Easter when I was fourteen, God shined down on me, and I got to go shopping for something new at my dad's store. Rich's department store was known for its beautiful Christmas tree that lit up the sky in downtown Atlanta. We watched every year on TV. The beautiful lobby areas, lovely mannequins, and amazing displays were beyond my discount store norms. Even though I had been in Rich's before, this time was special. I was old enough to appreciate the beauty.

As I entered the junior girl's clothing department, I was distracted by all the nice clothes. I couldn't imagine having the money to wear such fancy clothes on a normal Tuesday. My mom motioned for me to look at the pretty dresses that were close to the dressing room. I instantly saw things that I thought were lovely: a striped drop waist sailor dress, a floral puffy-sleeved dress, and a blue dress with a large, white bib collar with delicate crocheted lace edging. I quickly looked at the price tags, scouring the racks to find the cheapest price.

Out of the corner of my eye, I saw my dad walking toward the junior department. He was on his dinner break. After chatting for a moment, he asked if I had found anything I liked. I quickly showed him the three dresses I had found, and he matter-of-factly told me to go try my favorite dress on. I grabbed the sailor dress and ran to the dressing room. When I exited the dressing room to model for my parents, I was surprised to find my dad had returned to his department for work. His break was over. My mom nearly squealed with delight as she saw me looking pretty in the sweet dress. I knew this would be the one I was going to get. I didn't need to try anything else on. I was in love. If the price was right, this dress was going home with me.

But my mom had other ideas. Although she loved the sailor dress, she said I should try on the other two dresses just to be sure it was my favorite. I obeyed and just as eagerly modeled the floral dress and the blue bib dress. They were all so beautiful and fit perfectly. How was I going to make a choice?

I changed, gathered the dresses, and walked out of the dressing room, knowing I had to make a choice. It was going to be the sailor dress. I had wanted one like this for so long. It was meant to be.

But as I approached my mom, she reached for all the dresses. I knew. They were just too much. Even with the discount my dad would get, it was still too much money. We would wait a little longer, watch for sales, and eventually I would get a new dress. It was for the best.

But to my surprise she headed to the sales desk. As we approached the desk the smiling saleslady reached for the dresses.

"We will take all of these." My mom handed over all three of the dresses. The look on my face must have been utter shock, because my mom reached over and gently squeezed my hand. Then she reached for a crisp one-hundred-dollar bill and handed it to the lady behind the cash register to pay for my three new Sunday dresses. I was amazed, thrilled, excited, proud, thankful, happy, and humbled. I had never had three pretty new dresses at the same time. I didn't know how to handle the extravagant abundance.

How often I am reminded of this story. God's abundance has been a reoccurring theme in my life. But sometimes I miss it, because I am not paying attention. It doesn't always come in the form of possessions or money. Sometimes it's a beautiful sunrise, the smell of something that triggers a good memory, a cheerful note in the mail, or a hug from someone special. We sometimes take for granted the little ways God shows up and gives us more than we need or deserve. Much like the three dresses, sometimes he gives me more than I need at one time. He looks at what I need and instead of barely providing or just taking care of me, he says, "Give her everything! All that and more."

He's even doing it now! God is preparing an extravagant place of abundance for all those who know him.

Stop and Reclaim

And God is able to make all grace abound to you, so that having all sufficiency in all things at all times, you may abound in every good work. (2 Corinthians 9:8)

Every good gift and every perfect gift is from above, coming down from the Father of lights, with whom there is no variation or shadow due to change. (James 1:17)

Reclaim Today

How have you experienced the generosity of God?

_____

_____

_____

_____

_____

Three-Point Shot

I was in seventh grade when my parents removed my brother, sister, and I from our local Christian school. I was thirteen years old. They planned to homeschool us for the rest of our school years. They assured us we were not the only ones on this new adventure and began telling us of other families we knew that would be doing the three R's from their kitchen tables too. This was somewhat of a relief.

What I didn't know was that the small, misfit, community basketball team that I had played for the previous year planned to transfer to a homeschool league the next school year. I was so thrilled to hear I would still be able to play, and that our competition would include area schools, not just the B teams.

We began practices as soon as we could, borrowing local gyms and even a park basketball court. Coach Estes had us running laps, doing dribble drills, and shooting foul shots for what seemed like hours. I learned to sweat and like it. I was gaining confidence and finding out I liked being part of a team. Notice I never said I was a good athlete. I worked hard, ran the drills, and did my best, but I was not gifted. At 5'2", I could hit a free throw when uninhibited, make a layup if no one was blocking me, and take a block foul as good as anyone. However, please don't put me in the game thinking I can score points or make the tie-breaking basket. I was unreliable.

On one particular Saturday, at Forest Hills Christian School, we were fighting hard for a victory. I remember it like it was yesterday. Our team had yet to win a game. No matter how hard we tried we just didn't have the skills yet. But on this Saturday we were feisty. We were stealing, running the ball, and even hitting a few baskets. The score was close, and the minutes on the clock were few. I remember the coach gathering us together in a timeout encouraging us to slow down, think before we took a shot, and look for the open player. All of us girls stood there panting, out of breath, guzzling down water. We reentered the game to show them who was in charge.

We played hard. The score was separated by just two points. And, out of nowhere, someone threw the ball to me. Immediately I noticed no one was guarding the basket. I turned, dribbled to the three-point line, still unguarded. With yelling from fans and coaches and teammates, I shot the ball into the hoop with a swish.

In slow motion, the next scene played out.

The gym went instantly silent.

I looked at my coach. His red head, buried in his hands, shook back and forth. The referee blew his whistle and announced, "Three points for FHS!" And that's when I realized it. I had made three points in the wrong basket. No wonder no one was guarding me. No wonder the basket was wide open. No wonder the fans were screaming.

And there I stood. Embarrassed. Mortified.

I remember the ride home and my parents trying to take away the sting of the incident. The familiar quotes. "One basket doesn't win or lose a game" . . . "It could happen to anyone" . . . "There'll be other games" . . . But what I was hearing from myself was, "Loser" . . . "Idiot" . . . "How could you?"

As I've grown into adulthood, I've struggled with failure just like everyone else. I think I know what I am doing and realize, nope, that's not it. I head one direction and find out that's not the road for me. I hear the fans cheering and realize they aren't cheering for my success but for their own personal victories. I hear those failure words, "Idiot" . . . "Loser" . . . "Look at you" . . . just like I was in eighth grade again.

I wish getting older erased all the junior high drama we face as adults. The uncertainty, the vulnerability, the pressure—it's all still there. How we face defeat and victory tells a lot about what we are claiming as our source of strength. We can know the plays, run the drills, and even make the baskets, but we can still get it wrong. When we fail, we have the choice to listen to that negative, degrading talk of the enemy, or we can dig deeper and listen to that voice of truth, the one that says, "Forgiven" . . . "Try again" . . . "Grow stronger" . . . "Aim higher" . . . "Set goals" . . ."I love you" . . .

And even if we lose, we win. Because of our Victor, we win. We win when we catch the truth of who we are in Christ. Yes, we fail and make mistakes. We burn the cookies, shoot the ball into the wrong hoop, or say the wrong thing. But in Christ, we are victorious when we lean back into him and try again. We can block the voice of the enemy and stop the foul conversations and self-talk. The only talk we should be listening to is our Head Coach. We may not play the game of life perfectly, but we will grow from our mistakes and victories.

I'm happy to report that the East Metro Atlanta Christian

Homeschoolers stuck together for our entire high school basketball careers. By the time we were juniors, Christian and public schools were fearful of our amazing skills. We won homecoming trophies from private schools that had once laughed at our uniforms and our families. In the end we were victors. We had learned to play the game. We had learned from our coach that those laps around the gym and dribbling drills were all part of our strength training. They were part of us learning to work hard, to be a team, and to listen to the coach. They were all part of the victory.

Stop and Reclaim

But thanks be to God, who gives us the victory through our Lord Jesus Christ. (1 Corinthians 15:57)

For God gave us a spirit not of fear but of power and love and self-control. (2 Timothy 1:7)

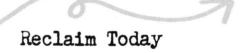

Reclaim Today

How do you recover from embarrassing mistakes? How should you recover from past mistakes?

_____

_____

_____

Five-Year-Old Lessons

He sat bright-eyed and excited on the tall piano bench. His legs dangled, not even close to reaching the floor beneath him. His fingers reached for the keys in a moment of curiosity. Quickly, his fingers tested each and every key. Then he looked at me with a grin, giddy to begin his first piano lesson.

We opened the beginner book and looked at pictures illustrating how he should sit at the piano. We traced his hands and labeled the fingers with numbers, so he would understand the importance of knowing which fingers to play. We found sets of black notes, and we pecked the keys with our thumbs like a rooster would with his beak. And then he said, "When am I gonna play the music?" His big eyes were anxious for my answer.

I replied, "We have to learn some basics before we can play the notes on the lines, but it won't be long!" Disappointment came over his eyes, and my heart melted a little. He must have imagined himself playing something beautiful after this first lesson.

It was so sweet and precious. His desire to play the piano was so admirable. In my heart I knew that I could rush him, but in the end he would end up frustrated and overwhelmed. I reminded myself it's better to learn one step at a time. He's eager. It wouldn't be too long before he's ready for music he could recognize.

Sometimes I find myself in the same boat. I want to be further along than I am. I want to be more than I am today. I want to rush out of this lesson that God is teaching me and get on with life or something easier. All the rushing through may be easier for the moment but not at the expense of learning the hard lessons in the times of waiting and building solid foundations.

> That next thing he has for you may depend on you learning what you need to in the present.

No one likes to wait. Not me, not five-year-old piano students, and not even you. Waiting is boring. We may not see the need. We might question God. But there is work to be done in the waiting. The waiting develops patience and improves our listening skills. The waiting teaches us perseverance, steadfastness, and self-discipline. The waiting proves whether or not you're ready for the next "God thing."

Don't grow weary in the waiting. When you don't understand God's purpose or his plan, don't worry. Lean in and listen with hopeful expectation. That next thing he has for you may depend on you learning what you need to in the present. We don't know if the next thing is good or bad. Perhaps this waiting season is to help strengthen you for a battle down the road. Maybe this waiting season is making the way for a bright future. We have choices regarding how we handle these times of waiting for the next thing: pout, sulk, wish it away, dread it, embrace it, or learn from it. As children of a good Father, let's learn what we need to learn in each season. Let's remind ourselves that God sees the big picture and knows exactly what lessons we need to equip us to play beautiful music.

Stop and Reclaim

Wait for the Lord; be strong, and let your heart take courage; wait for the Lord! (Psalm 27:14)

For you have need of endurance, so that when you have done the will of God you may receive what is promised. (Hebrews 10:36)

Reclaim Today

When have you had to wait on God? How did you handle it?
What lessons did you learn while you were waiting?

_____

_____

_____

_____

_____

_____

_____

_____

_____

_____

_____

Hateful Messages

I've wrestled today with thoughts of the past, mainly past hurts. It seems I can't get my mind to shut off. I'm remembering cruel text messages, lies, and hurtful words from people I once respected. I'm disappointed.

Today, for some reason my hurt was focused on one individual. One. One single person had power over my thoughts, my mind, and my focus for hours today. I replayed the message of the hateful text over and over in my mind. I struggled to even understand how someone who is so respected could be so hateful and full of spite. I still don't understand.

I wonder now, years later, how much time I have wasted replaying those hurtful, hateful, snarky words. And I don't want to waste those minutes again. At the end of today, as I type these words, I want it to be over, to quit rehashing, to quit letting it eat up my heart space. I want to forgive, leave it behind and be over it. Why is that so hard? Why is it so difficult to let go of the hurts of yesterday?

There is something in me that rationalizes that the sin committed against me is worse than the sins I commit every day. And guess what? It isn't. I have been forgiven of so much. Those same words that I have received are words that I have said or felt or acted on before too. Yet, somehow when I focus on the sin of others against me, I choose to forget the extreme and abundant grace that has covered those sins and mine. I find myself justifying and rationalizing my sins. And in those moments of hurt and anger I even find myself taking it out on others too. My family has been the brunt of more than one frustrating retaliation.

> The playing field is level through the lens of salvation.

This, my friend, is where the truth lies. It is snuggled between the pages of Scripture. 1 Timothy 1:15 says, "The saying is trustworthy and deserving of full acceptance, that Christ Jesus came into the world to save sinners, of whom I am the foremost." Paul admits that he is the number one sinner. But guess what? That's not the point of this verse. The point is this: Jesus came to save sinners like you and me, even the one who sent the hateful and hurtful text message. Even the one who gossips behind your back.

Even the one who intentionally seeks to destroy you. Their sin and my own sin are equal at the foot of the cross.

So how do I let go? It's a daily struggle. Focusing on the grace I've been given for the entirety of my sin helps me give less of my time and my heart to the hurts of the past. I don't always get this right, but I want my days of reclaiming to be more than my days of hurt. I will keep fighting for forgiveness. Grace helps me see past my own self to the forgiveness I have experienced because of God's gift of salvation. Grace keeps giving and receiving.

Stop and Reclaim

The saying is trustworthy and deserving of full acceptance, that Christ Jesus came into the world to save sinners, of whom I am the foremost. (1 Timothy 1:15)

Bearing with one another and, if one has a complaint against another, forgiving each other; as the Lord has forgiven you, so you also must forgive. (Colossians 3:13)

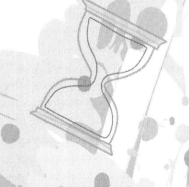

Reclaim Today

Have you been tempted to retaliate when someone speaks negativity into your life? Do you rehash the hurt? How can God's forgiveness toward you help move you toward forgiveness with others?

_____

_____

_____

_____

_____

_____

_____

_____

_____

_____

Messed-Up World

We mourn over more than just death. Gut-wrenching, stomach-turning, heart-aching situations can, in an instant, change everything. One phone call can change a day.

An affair, betrayal, wayward children, cancer, emotional distress . . . (insert your own issue here). In one moment, life can derail us. Families destroyed, jobs lost, hearts breaking—all because of one thing.

This world is messed up. We don't have to turn on the news to see it. It's not that far-removed. It's all around us, our homes, and our churches. And it's in us.

It's sin. It's pride. It's the lust for the now and the ignorance of what's to come.

Our world is living in the now, with little thought given for short lives, long eternities, and life beyond what we can see. Our temporal focus persuades us to believe the most urgent things are happening right before our eyes. We buy into the lies that the enemy wants us to believe. We forget about a glorious future waiting for us beyond this life. We forget the great price that has been paid.

But what if we took the time? What if we looked beyond today's date, today's forecast, today's agenda? What if we looked toward eternity with our hearts?

How would things look different? Would we take time to make better choices? Would there be moments to consider alternative plans and actions instead of accepting whatever media feeds us? Could there be moments of reconciliation instead of the deafening sounds of pride and arrogance?

> Our world is living in the now, with little thought given for short lives, long eternities, and life beyond what we can see.

God purify our hearts! Let's check our motives, our plans, our sinful nature, and our agendas against the holiness of God's Word and against eternity. Does God's Word give us direction? Will this matter in eternity? My friend, God does not leave us to be ignorant. His instructions are unchanging at a time in history when everything else seems to be changing. We can trust him, his words, and his promises—over and over again.

Instead of satisfying earthly desires, a child of God has the privilege of measuring our choices against the eternal calendar.

Before I choose my sin, I can weigh it against the truth of God's word. Before I choose my attitude, I can check to see if it lines up with the fruit of the Spirit. Before I make a decision, I can go to the Bible and get understanding, wisdom, and discernment. I can live in a constant state of eternity in my mind and heart. God gives us what we need through the truth of the Bible.

Dear God, you have overcome death, the grave, and the sin of yesterday, today, and forever. Help us to embrace you, the power, the hope, the only answer to every problem we will ever have. Teach us to cling tightly to your hand, the hand that can hold it all together. Purify us and put eternity in our hearts.

Stop and Reclaim

Little children, you are from God and have overcome them, for he who is in you is greater than he who is in the world. (1 John 4:4)

He has made everything beautiful in its time. Also, he has put eternity into man's heart, yet so that he cannot find out what God has done from the beginning to the end. (Ecclesiastes 3:11)

Reclaim Today

How can you focus on eternity more in your daily walk
with Christ?

_____

_____

_____

_____

_____

_____

_____

_____

_____

_____

_____

Overcoming Failure

I didn't menu plan for this week. I usually take time on Saturday to peruse Pinterest or at least flip through my *Taste of Home* magazine stash. Sometimes I'll call my mom for a recipe. This past Saturday I spent the morning at Costco, which might have you thinking, "Why didn't you pick up groceries then?" Well, it's because I am a failure. I was overwhelmed, and it was crowded, and I didn't have a list, and I wasn't sure what was a good buy and what wasn't. However, I did manage to walk away with four pounds of bacon. Priorities, right?

Now here we are a few days later. I am eating a cookie with dried-up decorations on it. Yes, it's gross. Tucker, my son, just ate a second bowl of cereal, and I'm pretty sure Savannah, my daughter, just drank the pickle juice out of the jar. Epic fail.

Bruce is picking up Dairy Queen on the way home. I'm going to eat my feelings of failure and drown my sorrows in a cheeseburger and greasy tater tots.

What do you do when you think you're a failure?

I've tried nearly everything to recover from failure before . . .

Eat my way out.

Cry my eyes out.

Hide out.

Shout out.

Honestly, I know all those things feel good for a little bit. But ultimately, they don't fix anything.

Try these tips the next time you're feeling like a loser:

Sift the truth from the failure. Could you have planned better, acted better, done better?

There's always room to grow . . . always room to improve.

Throw away the lies. What didn't you have control over? What was out of your hands? What is the enemy feeding you that isn't true?

Use the truth to make a better decision next time. What does God's Word say about it?

Forgive yourself and forgive others.

And while menu planning isn't going to make the world stop turning, there have been other failures in my life where I needed to take a serious look, so they didn't happen again. I've had to forgive myself when it was easier to beat myself up. I've had to examine the feelings of failure and reject the lies, "You're not a good enough menu planner, mom, wife, daughter, sister, friend, . . ." I've decided to use the truth to walk upright, with confidence that better days are ahead. No, we aren't starting a steady diet of pickle juice and stale cookies. Meat and veggies are in the near future. I am not the worst mom in the world.

And while I jest about much of this, isn't this true for the times of real defeat? There's nothing better that the devil wants than for us to be down for the count, defeated, and deflated, because we failed. Newsflash! I'm going to fail. So are you. So are your children, your boss, your husband, and your parents. Know that God has a purpose in allowing the failure. What is it? Growth. There's always room to grow. There's always room to improve. There's always room to get closer to the One with all the answers.

And meanwhile . . . Dairy Queen for dinner is not the worst thing that can happen.

Stop and Reclaim

But grow in the grace and knowledge of our Lord and Savior Jesus Christ. To him be the glory both now and to the day of eternity. Amen. (2 Peter 3:18)

Therefore, as you received Christ Jesus the Lord, so walk in him, rooted and built up in him and established in the faith, just as you were taught, abounding in thanksgiving. (Colossians 2:6–7)

Reclaim Today

Do you need to forgive yourself for a past failure? Write a note of reconciliation to yourself.

_____

_____

_____

_____

_____

_____

_____

_____

_____

_____

_____

_____

Whys

There have been many times in my life where I have asked God, "Why?"

Why did you take my dad to heaven when he was only forty-five?

Why did we struggle with infertility?

Why did you allow our daughter to be born at twenty-seven weeks?

Why did you allow a dear young man we loved to die in a tragic accident?

Why? Why? Why?

And then, just recently, I realized the only time I was ever asking "why?" was when bad things were happening. What about all the good that's happened?

Why did you bless me with such amazing parents?

Why have you provided so generously for my family throughout the years?

Why did I get to be a mom when other women never get the opportunity?

Why did you call me to serve you?

Why did you save me?

Why? Why? Why?

Why? Why? Why? It certainly sounds different asking God "why?" over the pleasant things that happen versus the unpleasant. Putting things into perspective with God's blessings challenges me to look at things through the lens of his Word.

Matthew 5:45 says, "For he makes his sun rise on the evil and on the good, and sends rain on the just and on the unjust."

> We aren't exempt
> from suffering.

We aren't exempt from suffering. I was reminded of this recently and was challenged to feel the suffering, not to shove it into the deep hole of my heart, but to really embrace it and learn from it. To feel it. Don't misunderstand. I am not sitting around asking for a double portion of suffering! In fact, I'm not sure that I even comprehend what suffering really is when I compare myself to most people in this world. But I am going to try to learn from the suffering that God allows to come my way. When the "whys" become less and the praise becomes more, then I will know I have touched the hem of this verse:

> *Not only that, but we rejoice in our sufferings, knowing that suffering produces endurance.* (Romans 5:3)

I'll be better trained to go the distance with Christ. Thank God for his amazing grace that puts all things into perspective.

Stop and Reclaim

Who has spoken and it came to pass, unless the Lord has commanded it? Is it not from the mouth of the Most High that good and bad come? Why should a living man complain, a man, about the punishment of his sins? (Lamentations 3:37–39)

Not only that, but we rejoice in our sufferings, knowing that suffering produces endurance. (Romans 5:3)

Reclaim Today

Make a list of five good things that God has allowed to happen in your life. Give thanks for those things, pondering the "why" of his goodness.

_____

_____

_____

_____

_____

_____

_____

_____

_____

_____

Hanging On

*S*econd guessing. We all do it—in our relationships, in our careers, in our speech, in our diets, in our parenting. We are so worried we won't get it right. We wrestle with the defeated life, past mistakes, and worried futures. We crave control.

But in the midst of all our anxiety and control issues, God says, "Let me."

Let me—

Be the one to decide your relationships.

Be the one to give you words to say.

Be the one to show you when to say those words.

Be the one to show you how to guide your children.

Be the one to love you with an everlasting love.

Be the one you trust when things go wrong, or you're disappointed, lonely, and feeling insecure . . .

And in those midnight hours when we are eyes-wide-open, we can learn to experience that "Let God" peace. It's a process. It's hard.

It's a bit humbling to know that the process of all things working together requires surrender on my part. God doesn't need my help to work things out. He wants my cooperation. When my kids were younger and wanted to help in the kitchen, I would pull up the step stool and have them watch what I was doing. I would demonstrate the measuring and mixing and they would watch. But inevitably, one of them would ask, "Can I help?"

> Frustrating circumstances are clear indicators in my life of areas I have not totally surrendered to the Lord.

Depending on what I was making, sometimes that was an option. Other times, it was not. Sometimes the process was delicate—folding in, bread rising, taking something hot from the oven. Sometimes the process was dangerous and required oven mitts or testing a cake to see if it was done. I did everything I could to protect them in the process of learning to cook and bake. They wanted a front row seat. They wanted their hands in the dough. They wanted to be a part of the finished project. Sometimes that just wasn't possible. Sometimes they had to take a step back and let me do the work. Sometimes it was for their own protection.

Much like my own children, I try to put my hands in the

batter before God is finished with the project. Things don't turn out quite right when I refuse to let God be in control. I'm miles from the finish line (heaven), and I feel like most days I am walking two paces forward and stepping back one. But I'm trying to let God.

In all honesty, controlling life is too much for me. I can't juggle it without him. I've tried. I've failed. I need him—seems like more each day. Or maybe I am just continuing to learn inch by inch that life is easier that way . . . the "let God" way.

So many moments have been wasted on trying to figure everything out. Frustrating circumstances are clear indicators in my life of areas I have not totally surrendered to the Lord. My pride and desire for control often get the best of me, until I recall what a good God we have. He welcomes our mess and says, "Let me work this all together for your good. Let me work it out."

Stop and Reclaim

I sought the LORD, and he answered me and delivered me from all my fears. (Psalm 34:4)

And we know that for those who love God all things work together for good, for those who are called according to his purpose. (Romans 8:28)

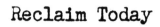

Reclaim Today

What do you need to "Let God" take over today?

_____

_____

_____

_____

_____

_____

_____

_____

_____

_____

_____

_____

_____

Scraps

I have a basket full of yarn that sits by my chair in the living room. Inside the basket you'll find all kinds of treasures: projects, crochet hooks, scissors, skeins of cotton yarn in various colors, and scraps. My scraps are small lengths of yarn that were too big to throw out, because surely they could be used for something!

I'm not a hoarder, but there's something like the possibility of creating something from the scraps that gets my creative juices flowing. There are all kinds of scraps: buttons, lace, fabric, chunks of wood, and, yes, yarn. I've seen people on YouTube and Instagram make masterpieces from their scraps. Surely mine will do the same.

Most of the time I'm a little disappointed in my attempts to be creative. It takes some careful thought and planning to put things together in a beautiful way. Sometimes I lose patience and just want it done. Sometimes I lack the skills needed to design the project. And sometimes I am just too lazy to give it the thought and planning it deserves.

I'm reminded that God works with scrappy pieces all the time. He takes all those leftovers that we think are no good, not enough, or slightly flawed, and he works them all together for our good. And he makes something beautiful. He makes something good out of the disappointments, mistakes, and hurts.

> There is a strange beauty that comes from using the scraps of our lives as an offering back to God.

Three years ago, I watched a young couple bury their only son after a tragic accident. It was, and still is, heart-wrenching. But yesterday I saw a glimmer of the masterpiece that God is creating. They knelt at the altar at church and prayed and wept with another young couple who just buried their one-month-old baby the day before. There is a strange beauty that comes from using the scraps of our lives as an offering back to God.

Nothing is wasted with the Lord. There is no part of our life that God cannot make into a beautiful masterpiece. Scraps and remnants are turned to masterpieces in the hands of the Master Crafter.

So, I've made a goal to use all the scrappy yarn I have, to make scrappy dishcloths this year. Each time I hook that yarn into the design, I am reminded that these little strings will be woven together to make something useful, helpful, and beautiful—just like God is using the broken pieces of my life.

Stop and Reclaim

As for you, you meant evil against me, but God meant it for good, to bring it about that many people should be kept alive, as they are today. (Genesis 50:20)

Reclaim Today

What scraps do you need to turn over to the Lord so he can make something beautiful?

_____

_____

_____

_____

_____

_____

_____

_____

_____

_____

_____

Empty Cupboards

Shortly after Bruce and I married, we were in need—a common occurrence among young married ministry couples. Church youth positions paid very little those days, and even with other jobs, the paychecks were unstable. And so were we.

I panicked one weekend when I realized we were down to our last canned goods. The paycheck I received for substitute teaching wouldn't be in the mail until the next week. The small forty-dollar check Bruce received from church was only enough to pay the water bill and put gas in the car. I was worried, embarrassed, and wondering how we would make it through the next week.

In his sermon series, *Keys to Crossing Over*, Steven Furtick says, "God knows how to feed you for every season you're in. He fed the Israelites pots of meat in Egypt, manna in the wilderness and gave them the land full of milk and honey in the promised land."[2]

That Sunday morning we served in our church, ate a sandwich

2 Steven Furtick, *Keys to Crossing Over*, sermon series, 2016, https://stevenfurtick. com/keys-to-crossing-over/.

for lunch, then returned to church late that afternoon. As we entered the church, a young rancher approached Bruce and asked him to come see something at his car. Bruce obliged, and I continued on into the church. A few minutes later Bruce met me in the hallway. He was a mix of tears and excitement.

"They just gave us a side of beef!" The words spilled out. "Can you believe it? A whole side of beef!"

Not being a native of Texas, I had no idea exactly what a side of

> God takes care of us ... It could be "just enough" or it could be in abundance.

beef looked like, but I knew it was food. We needed food, so that was good news to me! I hugged Bruce and later hugged the young rancher and his wife. I was overwhelmed that they had thought of us. I learned that day that a side of beef, was more meat than my freezer had ever seen at one time. That evening as we stuffed our upright refrigerator freezer, I could not have been more grateful for God's provision for us.

God takes care of us. It might not be the way we thought. It might be from an unexpected source. It could be "just enough" or it could be in abundance. It may mean we have to leave the bondage of Egypt and trust God in the wilderness. But that's just it. God is trustworthy. Whether it's food or something else, we can depend on our dependable God to provide for our needs.

Wherever we find ourselves, we can be confident that God will supply what we need, just as he did for the Israelites. It wasn't what they always wanted, but it was sufficient. It was enough, and only God knew it was exactly what they needed.

God's provision might come unexpectedly. It might be different from what I thought it would be, but he is God and he knows significantly more about my needs than I do.

That little interaction with the rancher back in Bryan, Texas, nearly twenty-five years ago, set me up for a lifetime of learning to trust God in moments of need and lack. He is not in the business of letting his children go without. In every season God knows just how to feed us.

Stop and Reclaim

Not that I am speaking of being in need, for I have learned in whatever situation I am to be content. (Philippians 4:11)

Reclaim Today

Do you find yourself needing something today? Remember a time that God has provided for you and use that experience to encourage your heart. He will provide again.

_____

_____

_____

_____

_____

_____

_____

_____

_____

_____

Forgotten

My daughter and I left early for church one evening, because we had an errand to run on the way there. My husband and son were going to travel separately and join us at church for a music rehearsal. The guys had been out golfing earlier and both needed to clean up before going to the church.

Savannah and I were already on stage when Bruce arrived. As he walked down the center aisle of the church, I wondered where Tucker had gone. Practice was starting soon, and I didn't want him walking in late. Just as I was about to ask, Bruce looked at me and asked, "Tucker's not with you?" I shook my head and laughed a little. No . . . Tucker wasn't with me.

Bruce had unintentionally left Tucker, our fourteen-year-old son, at home. Tucker had gone to his room after his shower and was listening to music on his headphones. He didn't hear Bruce call for him, so Bruce assumed he had changed his mind and hitched a ride with me. At home, Tucker sensed that it should have been time to leave already, looked out the french doors to our driveway, and realized he had been forgotten, left behind. Quickly he had texted his dad, who by then, was already on his way home to get him.

Feeling forgotten isn't a good feeling. Feeling like no one cares or is concerned for your well-being is defeating and heavy.

> Feeling like no one cares or is concerned for your well-being is defeating and heavy.

God has never forgotten you. The gospel is a beautiful display of his remembrance of mankind. While we forgot about him, he remembered us. Think back to years ago when God created a beautiful garden of perfection for Adam and Eve. Not too long after, mankind became curious, proud, and disobedient. Thinking they knew what was best, they arrogantly threw away the gift of the garden, the sweet fellowship with God, and in a moment, sin covered the earth.

God had a plan to restore mankind. He had not forgotten us. Nearly 2000 years later, he gave us his perfect Son to be born as a baby and horrifically sacrificed as our Savior.

God didn't forget us. We hadn't slipped his mind.

From the garden to the cross to today, he has always known just what we needed. Even when we tried to do our own thing or thought we knew what was best, he made a way for us. Mary, Joseph, and the manger were the means to bring Jesus to be born and to die. God knew we needed saving, so he gave us a Savior. He knew we needed hope, so he gave us a resurrected Savior. He knew one day we would need deliverance from this hard world, so he gave us a coming Savior, a King. He has never forgotten us.

And for all the in-between times, he knows what you need: hurts healed, health restored, employment found, bills paid, families mended, kindness received, love given. Every day he is remembering us as he meets our needs.

So, when you are feeling like you've been left behind, be reassured that God has not forgotten you.

Stop and Reclaim

But you are a chosen race, a royal priesthood, a holy nation, a people for his own possession, that you may proclaim the excellencies of him who called you out of darkness into his marvelous light. (1 Peter 2:9)

Reclaim Today

Look around. Are there people in your life that might feel forgotten? Reach out. Let them know what you know: God never forgets his children. Write a prayer for them below.

_____

_____

_____

_____

_____

_____

_____

_____

_____

_____

_____

Laundry Service

$\mathcal{I}$n September of 2019, teams from Texas, Louisiana, Georgia, Oklahoma, and Alabama were servicing those who had been devastated by Tropical Storm Imelda. These Baptist Disaster Teams left us far better than they found us. They pulled insulation, tore out sheetrock, ripped up flooring, and so much more. They navigated many residents through phase one of a huge, soggy mess.

The Louisiana team won my heart, because they brought the laundry man, Mr. Johnson. Have you ever met a person who you enjoy from the start? That was Mr. Johnson. He was fun, kind, soft-spoken, spiritual, and relevant. And he washed the laundry— load after load.

About that laundry . . . it wasn't your ordinary laundry that he was servicing. It was moldy, mildewy, drenched, and stench-filled. Blankets mopped up sewage water. Towels soaked by the muddy waters from overflowing canals, ditches and toilets piled high each day as load after load was dropped off. It was sweaty, smelly, and messy. It was covered with disintegrated pieces of sheetrock and insulation. Disgusting socks, undies, and t-shirts that filled large laundry baskets should probably have filled dumpsters instead. There was baby laundry, teenage-boy laundry, and bathroom laundry. All had one common factor—it reeked!

> The stinky days will come, but remembering who we serve will help our work become a sweet fragrance of worship to the Lord.

Mr. Johnson came in each week, stayed four or five days, then returned to his bride and church each weekend. Last fall, his church ordained him as a deacon. I don't have one doubt that he met every qualification. He served us in the humblest way. He met people at a time of greatest need and humbly cared for them. It was one less thing to worry about. Three fewer things to remember—wash, dry, and fold.

True service, the kind that ministers to others, is done the way Mr. Johnson did it. He had a smile on his face, kindness in his heart, and gentleness in his gestures as he dealt with people. Humility in every single action.

Mr. Johnson had his eyes on Jesus. There's no way you can mess with dirty laundry, day in and day out, with a good attitude all on your own (says every mother everywhere.) Mr. Johnson reminded me that our focus must stay on the Master in order to be an obedient and cheerful servant. The stinky days will come, but remembering who we serve will help our work become a sweet fragrance of worship to the Lord.

Stop and Reclaim

Serve the LORD with gladness! Come into his presence with singing! (Psalm 100:2)

For we are his workmanship, created in Christ Jesus for good works, which God prepared beforehand, that we should walk in them. (Ephesians 2:10)

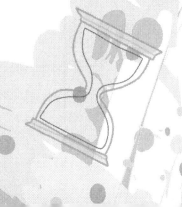

Reclaim Today

List the tasks you prefer not to do at home or work. How can you begin reclaiming those tasks as worship to the Lord?

_____

_____

_____

_____

_____

_____

_____

_____

_____

_____

_____

_____

Freeloading

The year was 2018. We were in the middle of a move. From our housing to our laundry services, from the care of our dog to the Wi-Fi access—we were experiencing almost everything at the hand and wallet of someone else. It was humbling to be on the receiving end of someone else's generosity. Someone else dealt with the expense and inconvenience to provide for my family while we waited to move into our home. It felt wonderful, awkward, overwhelming, and so very kind.

That generosity was coming from people who knew what it's like to be displaced. Hurricane Harvey had ravaged the area just a year before. Most people in our area were impacted. These were people who were still recovering, cleaning, helping, and rebuilding. These weren't people who had recovered completely. They were just people humbly helping people. Neighbor helping neighbor.

It was a picture-perfect example of how God's Word teaches us to be generous. God was generous in his gift of salvation. Various churches were generous to Paul. The widow was generous with her mite. Once we realize what we've been given spiritually, we can't help but overflow with generosity.

Over and over we see the lessons of generosity taught in Scripture. It's not just in material things; we are to be unselfish in our forgiveness, lavish in our love, and charitable in our encouraging words. We are to be overly kind, understanding, and helpful.

> These were people who were still recovering, cleaning, helping, and rebuilding.

In contrast, we are to be slow to wrath, hold back our anger, and spare others from harsh words. We are to rethink criticism and listen twice as much as we speak. Negative words carry a heavy weight, and we need to think before we attack.

The generous person has learned to give until it's second nature. They don't sit around calculating the cost of their generosity. They give without expecting anything in return. They realized and understood the generosity they have experienced. Our church members went above and beyond what was reasonable and were elaborate in their generosity. Their actions were a reflection of the generous work God had done in their hearts. When we truly understand what God has done for us, we become generous in every way.

Maybe you're thinking that you don't have much to give materially. Friendship, a hug, a welcoming presence, an act of service—we all have some way we can be generous. Think about how God has gifted you and find a way to pass a little of that generously on to someone else.

I'm thankful we serve a generous God. I'm also thankful for the generous people who have blessed my family and me through the years. The biblical art of generosity is slowly fading with the rise of the "me first" attitude. As we study God's Word and learn to be more like him, we can become more generous with our words, kind deeds, financial giving, and helping those in need—even if that just means sharing your Wi-Fi with the preacher's wife!

Stop and Reclaim

By this we know love, that he laid down his life for us, and we ought to lay down our lives for the brothers. But if anyone has the world's goods and sees his brother in need, yet closes his heart against him, how does God's love abide in him? Little children, let us not love in word or talk but in deed and in truth. (1 John 3:16–18)

Reclaim Today

Make a short list of people you know who are in need. The need could be physical, spiritual, mental, or emotional. Pray, asking God to tender your heart toward a need you can help meet.

_____

_____

_____

_____

_____

_____

_____

_____

_____

_____

Refinish

*M*y dad was the best amateur woodworker I knew. He hand-crafted several beautiful pieces of furniture that have been passed down to me through the years. Some of my favorite pieces are not the ones he made, but the ones he restored. He could take a dingy old dresser, sand it down, smooth out the rough edges, and make a beautiful, useful piece of furniture. There was nothing that a good coat of paint couldn't fix.

I remember him restoring a four-poster bed and matching dresser that my grandparents left to my mom. The bed and dresser started out dusty and dirty, but with great care, my dad stripped them down to their natural color, gently removed and cleaned the hardware, restained the wood a natural cherry color, and put all the pieces back together. When restored, the pieces looked brand new, usable, attractive, and cared for.

Restoration. It's what God is all about. From our sinful state as unrighteous and filthy rags, to forgiven and redeemed believers, transformation has always been his business.

And why? For his glory! We cannot boast of how we have washed ourselves clean. We cannot brag about what we have done. It is all only for his ultimate glory!

Do you have something in your life that needs restoration: a relationship, a habit, an attitude? God can make what some consider a heap of useless junk and make something beautiful. He wants to take the bits of your life—the scrap wood, the discarded antiques you have piled in the corner and called broken—and he wants to raise something better from the rubble. For his glory.

Can we let go of the ugly and let him do some restoring? Can we trust him with the special places in our hearts? Can we believe he will reclaim them? Can we give him control? Could we, day by day, allow him to reclaim the shattered pieces of our lives and create something of beauty?

When we give him permission to sand down our rough edges, to strip away the calluses of our hearts, and to see all the raw hurt and pain, he can refinish us and make us new.

What glory that would bring him! When we give him permission to sand down our rough edges, to strip away the calluses of our hearts, and to see all the raw hurt and pain, he can refinish us and make us new. He is always looking for those who are willing to go through the refinishing process.

Stop and Reclaim

To grant to those who mourn in Zion—to give them a beautiful headdress instead of ashes, the oil of gladness instead of mourning, the garment of praise instead of a faint spirit; that they may be called oaks of righteousness, the planting of the LORD, that he may be glorified. (Isaiah 61:3)

He has made everything beautiful in its time. Also, he has put eternity into man's heart, yet so that he cannot find out what God has done from the beginning to the end. (Ecclesiastes 3:11)

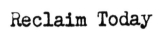

Reclaim Today

What area in your life do you need to reclaim for the glory of God?
What has the enemy destroyed that God wants to use for good?

_____

_____

_____

_____

_____

_____

_____

_____

_____

_____

_____

Do-Overs

*E*veryone needs a fresh start.

The prodigal child

The distant spouse

The bored housewife

The drug addict

The overeater

The proud

The angry

The disrespectful

Everyone needs a fresh start.

Let's be real. There's been a time in each of our lives when we needed a do-over. January is a good place to get one. Everyone is busy doing their own self-examinations. We analyze our lives and write down new, more attainable goals. It's like a fresh page in a book, or a newly painted wall—clean, spacious, perfect.

We have the momentum to be anything, do anything, and

achieve anything, because we have a fresh start. That feeling of rockstardom, I-believe-I-can-fly mentality sends adrenaline pumping through our veins like coffee on a cold winter's day. We are unstoppable.

For about five minutes. That's when it happens. One of the kids spills his cereal, husband can't find his keys, you're sure you had your phone in the bedroom, the dog ate the backyard furniture, the garbage disposal smells like rotten eggs, and any hope of you being Superwoman goes down the drain. Your clean page is now spotted with Cheerios and smells like egg salad.

And that's why I love this verse:

> *His mercies never come to an end; they are new every morning.* (Lamentations 3:23)

Because we all need a New Year's Day more than once a year. In fact, some of us need one every day! And isn't it just like the Lord to know that his mercy would be just what we need to get through each day—not just on New Year's Day! See, Supermom gets this lavish mercy extended to her just like the prodigal son or daughter. And that man who cut you off in traffic needs new mercy just like your grandmother. No one is immune. We all need it!

New mercy looks beyond the failed effort and sees straight to the heart.

I don't even want to think of all the times I've started diets, made goals to read my Bible all the way through, written down other resolutions—only to be sidetracked. Guilt can set in pretty quickly when you realize you're on your fifth or sixth failure in that many days. The best menu plans, goal sheets, and habit trackers all seem to laugh in your face when you fail. Thank God for new mercy.

New mercy looks beyond the failed effort and sees straight to the heart. Like a father who knows his children, new mercy sees the effort, sees the intention, and sees the soul. He knows that although our goals and plans may be lofty and award-winning, we will always fail without new mercy.

So, next time (probably today or tomorrow), when you feel the pangs of exasperation flooding your soul, when plans haven't gone according to the planner, or when you're feeling depleted, embrace the mercy for that day—the new mercy—measured out in the perfect dose for you and me.

Stop and Reclaim

The steadfast love of the Lord never ceases; his mercies never come to an end; they are new every morning; great is your faithfulness. (Lamentations 3:22–23)

Therefore, if anyone is in Christ, he is a new creation. The old has passed away; behold, the new has come. (2 Corinthians 5:17)

Reclaim Today

Do you need a New Year's Day do-over? Have you made a goal and let it fall by the wayside? Commit to making a step in that direction today. It's not too late.

_____

_____

_____

_____

_____

_____

_____

_____

_____

_____

_____

Death

She welcomed me into the family with a warmth and authenticity I had never experienced before. She was a white-haired, stout-figured, smiling lady who in a few short months would become my mother-in-law. Together, through the next twenty-six years, we would enjoy cooking, shopping, reminiscing, looking at photos, and playing with her grandkids. She would fiercely defend her family, spoil us too much at Christmas, and tell you I was her favorite child.

Until she couldn't. It started slowly—something innocently forgotten, a wrong name, a missing ingredient in a recipe. Then there was the day she called her son by her late husband's name. On another day she called 911 just to chat with the police. And another day she left the stove on. We didn't need a doctor's diagnosis. We knew. We knew she was the recipient of the dreaded memory-stealing disease of dementia. We knew we were losing her.

Sometimes death comes in quickly and steals the life at such a pace that even those who are alive have trouble catching their breath. I do not know which is worse, but I know that the slow, prolonged, sad death of the mind is a grief I had not experienced before. My friend, my mother-in-law, whose voice I can still hear clearly in my head, was gone before she was gone. Those last months of her life were our saddest. She was frustrated, and we were grieving. She was irritable, and we were grieving. As her last days became apparent, we cried for mercy, for her and for us.

> Sometimes death comes in quickly and steals the life at such a pace that even those who are alive have trouble catching their breath.

Death. It doesn't really matter how a person dies that catches our breath, it's that they're gone. We can analyze and compare stories of cancer and brain aneurysms, of organ failure and old age, and even of murder. The end result is the same. We are left with this feeling of empty, lonely purposelessness.

Death strikes. We are never prepared enough. We can't be ready enough. When that last breath is drawn, you realize it won't be followed by another raising of the chest and an exhale. No amount of preparation, of God-knowledge, of eternal perspective is enough for that first moment without the one you love. Its heavy thickness is near strangulation strength.

And then you remember. It may take a moment, or a few

months of moments—even years—but your mind finally compre-hends and shifts to the beautiful hope we have in Christ. It's that hope that we will be with our Christian loved ones once again, that this is not the end. This world is not the final stop.

There is hope:

- the resurrection hope that we can cling to in the worst of times,
- the hope that we have in a glorious future that he's prepared for us in eternity,
- the hope of his soon return,
- the hope that believes he keeps his promise,
- the hope that does not leave us lonely but filled with the beautiful reality that we are not alone as we walk in the day-to-day—in this weight of grief.

We have hope. Hope in him. Beautiful, beautiful hope. That same hope he promised 2000 years ago.

Stop and Reclaim

Precious in the sight of the Lord is the death of his saints. (Psalm 116:15)

O death, where is your victory? O death, where is your sting? (1 Corinthians 15:55)

Reclaim Today

Are you mourning the loss of someone you love? How can you embrace hope and the message of heaven during this time?

_____

_____

_____

_____

_____

_____

_____

_____

_____

_____

_____

_____

Routine

*D*o you ever wonder how your house gets so messy? Does it ever cross your mind just to take a huge backhoe and bury it all? Am I the only one who wonders if anyone else in the house can empty the dishwasher or smell the rancid trash? Sometimes the routine of motherhood and home-keeping can be tiring and frustrating. It's easy, so easy, to get an attitude. Believe me, I speak from a lot of experience with messes, and attitudes. In all the years of staying home, you'd think I would have the routine down by now.

I have a house that needs a lot of attention today. It's more than the usual mess. It's the put-on-the-gloves-and-perhaps-a-mask-and-dive-in kind of mess. I am slightly annoyed with myself that I've let it come to this.

So I have some choices:

    1) do the task before me to the best of my ability,

turn on some tunes, enjoy the process of reclaiming cleanliness and get 'er done,

OR

2) clean halfheartedly, complain, have a bad attitude, and make myself (and anyone I come into contact with) miserable.

One of these ways lends itself to worship. The other clearly does not. I have this opportunity daily, whether I am mopping floors or singing at church. I get to worship any day of the week, because my work, no matter what it is, can be part of my worship.

Ever wonder how your house gets so messy? Does it ever cross your mind just to take a huge backhoe and bury it all?

It's pretty much the choice we have every day as we get up and do whatever it is God has called us to do. Whether it's parenting, working our paid jobs, volunteering, marriage, or something else, God has something for you to do today. It might look like ordinary work, but anything that God calls us to do is holy work. We should do it with all our heart—with serving him in mind, not our boss, employer, or anyone else.

Ordinary work can set the stage for extraordinary worship. When the task is dreaded or difficult, we can decide this moment will be a moment of worship. The routine of toilet scrubbing, dish washing, and floor mopping can quickly be traded for the opportunity to sing, dance, and worship. That's an eternal trade that produces great benefits.

Worshipping in the routine of cleaning days, working days, school days, and all the days in between creates opportunities for God to be glorified. The world will wonder how we can exude such joy in the routine and ordinary. The world will see something greater than us, in us. That's the goal of worship in the routine.

So what's before you today—something you love or something you dread? It really doesn't matter. It's time to get to work, wholeheartedly, as we serve the Lord. Think of the smile it must bring to his face to see us working for his glory, even when it's difficult. We can do the hard things, serve the difficult people, and work with all our hearts to honor him. After all, didn't he do just that when he walked the earth?

Do something—

With your whole heart—

As if the Lord is right beside you (because he is!)

Now, I'm off to clean toilets.

Stop and Reclaim

Whatever you do, work heartily, as for the Lord and not for men. (Colossians 3:23)

Reclaim Today

What is a task you've been putting off? Can you tackle it today? Write yourself a procrastinator's checklist and mark those things off as you tackle them.

_____

_____

_____

_____

_____

_____

_____

_____

_____

_____

Chaos

*H*eading to bed last night, I thought about how tired I was. I thought through my schedule: a busy week, our spring ladies' event at church, Mother's Day, and an unexpected out-of-town trip. Well, you know how it is. We've all been there before. I was just plain, old tired.

To top it off, I was worried. My mother-in-law was sick to the point of death. We were all essentially just waiting for the call. I knew this would have a heart-wrenching effect on all of us, especially my kids, who adored her. While trying to sleep, my ear would be unintentionally listening to hear the ringing of the phone. It had been weeks since a good night's sleep.

Ironically, sometimes it seems when I am overly tired that I don't sleep well. But Jeremiah 31:25 has a wonderful message. God will refresh the weary, the tired, the worn out, the exhausted. But he doesn't stop there. In addition to refreshing us, he says he will satisfy or replenish the faint (grieving).

Life can throw us curveballs that leave us sleepless, anxious, and worried. But here God says, "I'm going to refresh you. I'm going to take all the things that are crying out for your attention, those things that keep you up at night, those things that have you unsettled, those things that are grieving your heart, and I'm going to take them on myself." It's the New Testament equivalent of bearing your burdens. He continues, "In exchange, you can be refreshed and satisfied in me." What a deal for us!

> Are you concerned or worried about something? Take it to the Lord.

My problems might not go away—that issue with a co-worker or wayward child might not be resolved—but I can rest easy knowing God is refreshing my spirit. He is satisfying my needs. He is equipping me with what I need to face the future. What a comfort to a tired soul.

He is waiting on us to turn over the control to him. In the midst of chaotic days and sleepless nights, he lovingly offers refreshment and rest. So many times we look to other places and techniques to find this soul rest. Vacations, hobbies, grandkids, shopping, binge watching—while not necessarily bad in and of themselves—they are poor substitutes from the rest and refreshment that comes from the Lord. The rest the Lord gives brings hope and peace. We can face the next thing or the next day because he has provided refreshment for our souls.

Rest is good for our body and our souls. From birth, doctors tell mothers to be sure their children get a good night's rest. Rest helps children grow. Rest prepares the body to function at its best. Rest helps us to recover from hard days. Rest is good.

The rest God gives is even better.

Are you concerned or worried about something? Take it to the Lord. His Word tells us he never sleeps, so why not let him take your anxious heart and solve your problems? He'll be up anyway!

Stop and Reclaim

I will refresh the weary and satisfy the faint. (Jeremiah 31:25)

Behold, he who keeps Israel will neither slumber nor sleep. (Psalm 121:4)

Reclaim Today

Are you worried about something you cannot control? Jot it down and tuck it in bed for the night. God is taking care of it.

_____

_____

_____

_____

_____

_____

_____

_____

_____

_____

_____

_____

Change

*C*hapters end.
Doors close.

Seasons change.

Life goes on.

Sometimes we are prepared for the changes, and sometimes we are not.

All the preparing in the world can't ready you for the loss of a job, a cancer diagnosis, the death of a spouse, a fire raging through your home, or the rebellion of a child. Nothing readies you for the permanence of death or the tragedy of loss.

Sometimes change is a punch in the gut, a slap across the face, a rude wake-up call. Like being unprepared for the whip of freezing wind and temperatures in a January snowstorm, these changes frustrate and anger us. They come to devastate and manipulate, and there isn't one thing we can do. We are not in control.

What can we do when faced with the abrupt changes of life

that will inevitably come? Besides pitching a toddler tantrum, here are a few tips that get me through unpredictable changes:

First, we can count on the one who never changes to guide us. Hebrews 13:8 says, "Jesus Christ is the same yesterday and today and forever." When the world is crashing all around us, we can go to the trustworthy and stable force that is Jesus Christ. His dependability for all times has been tested. He has never failed.

Second, we can put on the armor of God. Ephesians 6:10–18 gives us head-to-toe wardrobe guidelines for defensive and offensive protection from the enemy. When we are feeling down because of our circumstances, we become a prime target for the enemy to defeat us. Wardrobe malfunctions can be a thing of the past, if we take the time to put on the armor of God. We can protect ourselves from the tactics of the enemy when we outfit ourselves in the armor.

> Wardrobe malfunctions can be a thing of the past, if we take the time to put on the armor of God.

Third, we can focus on the truth. Philippians 4:8 says,

Finally, brothers, whatever is true, whatever is honorable, whatever is just, whatever is pure, whatever is lovely, whatever is commendable, if there is any excellence, if there is anything worthy of praise, think about these things.

Keeping our thoughts and minds on the truth defeats the lies we are so susceptible to when we are overwhelmed. We should focus on the Word of God and what it says. We ought to give little thought to the careless words the devil might tempt us to believe. The devil tends to twist and turn the truth of God's words. We don't have to believe him. Let's go directly to the source of truth.

So whatever changes life is throwing your way today, decide now to trust in the unchanging Jesus, put on the armor and focus your thoughts. While these may not solve all your problems, these steps will calm your heart.

Stop and Reclaim

Jesus Christ is the same yesterday and today and forever. (Hebrews 13:8)

Finally, be strong in the Lord and in the strength of his might. Put on the whole armor of God, that you may be able to stand against the schemes of the devil. For we do not wrestle against flesh and blood, but against the rulers, against the authorities, against the cosmic powers over this present darkness, against the spiritual forces of evil in the heavenly places. Therefore, take up the whole armor of God, that you may be able to withstand in the evil day, and having done all, to stand firm. Stand therefore, having fastened on the belt of truth, and having put on the breastplate of righteousness, and, as shoes for your feet, having put on the readiness given by the gospel of peace. In all circumstances take up the shield of faith, with which you can extinguish all the flaming darts of the evil one; and take the helmet of salvation, and the sword of the Spirit, which is the word of God, praying at all times in the Spirit, with all prayer and supplication. To that end, keep alert with all perseverance, making supplication for all the saints. (Ephesians 6:10–18)

Finally, brothers, whatever is true, whatever is honorable, whatever is just, whatever is pure, whatever is lovely, whatever is commendable, if there is any excellence, if there is anything worthy of praise, think about these things. (Philippians 4:8)

Reclaim Today

How can you change your thinking to reflect Philippians 4:8? What piece of armor do you need to be sure to put on?

_____

_____

_____

_____

_____

_____

_____

_____

Control Issues

*A*re you a controller? A manipulator? Do you have to have the last word? Do you get angry when people don't play by your rules?

Let's be honest. Controllers and manipulators are everywhere—at our jobs, in our government, at our churches, and in some marriages. This was also a huge issue in the Bible.

Think about the children of Israel. They were always thinking they knew best instead of trusting God. They tried to manipulate their way all the way to the promised land, and it ended up setting them back about forty years.

Think about David, a master manipulator of all things involving Bathsheba and his adulterous affair. His manipulation landed him with a murder confession and an illegitimate child.

Think about Potiphar's wife who made false accusations about Joseph for flirtatious behavior. Think about Haman who hated Mordecai so much that he orchestrated gallows for his hanging.

Seriously! We could go on and on. Throughout the scriptures

these illustrations of dramatic manipulation of circumstances and control of people saturate the pages of God's Word. There must be some sort of guide or solution for dealing with such people and, if truth be told, in acting like such people.

2 Timothy 3:1–5 says,

> But understand this, that in the last days there will come times of difficulty. For people will be lovers of self, lovers of money, proud, arrogant, abusive, disobedient to their parents, ungrateful, unholy, heartless, unappeasable, slanderous, without self-control, brutal, not loving good, treacherous, reckless, swollen with conceit, lovers of pleasure rather than lovers of God, having the appearance of godliness, but denying its power. Avoid such people.

Avoid such people. Wow! Sounds pretty simple. Avoid them; go another route; take another path; minimize their influence; do what you can to not be around them. It could mean you are inconvenienced. It could mean you are lied about, laughed at, or considered a coward for going another way, but that's not walking in truth. And the truth says, "avoid such people."

When we allow others to control us, we leave no room for the Holy Spirit to control us.

Controllers and manipulators . . .

If you are one, David showed us exactly how to handle yourself. What did he do after he realized his arrogant sin? He acknowledged his pride, arrogance, and control issues. He confessed them before the Lord, and then went on to do right. Quit the behaviors that feed the addiction of power.

Try, instead, to serve in a place of humility. Try, instead, to love in a place of lowliness. Soon you will see people are much more willing to follow someone of a meek and serving spirit, someone who is spirit-controlled instead of self-appointed control.

What if you're the one being controlled and manipulated? Recognize the symptoms mentioned in 2 Timothy (lovers of self, lovers of money, proud, etc.) Every one of those characteristics indicates a controlling or manipulating tendency. While no one is perfect, we would be wise to discern who we are giving control over to and avoid those who fall into the habit of control and manipulation. When we allow others to control us, we leave no room for the Holy Spirit to control us. You can't serve two masters.

Stop and Reclaim

But understand this, that in the last days there will come times of difficulty. For people will be lovers of self, lovers of money, proud, arrogant, abusive, disobedient to their parents, ungrateful, unholy, heartless, unappeasable, slanderous, without self-control, brutal, not loving good, treacherous, reckless, swollen with conceit, lovers of pleasure rather than lovers of God, having the appearance of godliness, but denying its power. Avoid such people. (2 Timothy 3:1–5)

No one can serve two masters, for either he will hate the one and love the other, or he will be devoted to the one and despise the other. You cannot serve God and money. (Matthew 6:24)

See that no one leads you astray. (Matthew 24:4)

Reclaim Today

Do you feel controlled by someone? Using the verses above make a plan for what you will do the next time you are in their presence. How will you handle yourself?

_____

_____

_____

_____

_____

_____

_____

_____

_____

Motherhood

*W*atching children grow up in today's world can be frightening. The addictions, violence, and sexual indecencies (and so much more!) our children are exposed to from an early age should bring sadness to our souls.

Who will be the real mothers—the ones who will guard their children's hearts, hold their hands, set the example, protect their minds? Who will be the mothers who prioritize their own spiritual lives, stand for purity, sacrifice their desires, and build foundations on absolute truths? Who will be the real mothers who contradict culture, who pray, who read the Word of God and teach what it says? Who will be the mothers who teach young men and women that it's more important to love others than their own selfish desires and that real beauty comes from within? Who will be that mother?

You see, the world is full of women who can give birth to beautiful babies. The miracle of new life is so fresh from heaven, it's breathtaking. But it is duplicated thousands of times a day in hospitals, homes, and birthing centers. The ability to give birth is not unique to you or me or the next woman.

> Whether you've birthed children, adopted children, buried children, fostered children, or have a barren womb —you can be a spiritual mother.

What is unique is the ability to be a spiritual mom to this generation of searching young people. This rare form of mothering rises up, holds this generation in prayer, in the presence and the power of Jesus.

Declare that you will be that mother—
The advocate,
the protector,
the hope-giver,
the prayer warrior,
the foundation builder,
the truth seeker,
the loving example.
And that, my friend, has nothing to do with your biological

clock, your empty nest, your childless womb, or your empty arms.

It has to do with your heart, the mother heart God has given you. Whether you've birthed children, adopted children, buried children, fostered children, or have a barren womb—you can be a spiritual mother.

And I wonder, in this world today, if that's not what we really need more than anything. Will you be the one? The one who loves beyond the womb? Will you be that mother?

Stop and Reclaim

She opens her mouth with wisdom, and the teaching of kindness is on her tongue. (Proverbs 31:26)

To you the helpless commits himself; you have been the helper of the fatherless. (Psalm 10:14)

Religion that is pure and undefiled before God the Father is this: to visit orphans and widows in their affliction, and to keep oneself unstained from the world. (James 1:27)

Reclaim Today

Do you know a child or teen who could use a mother? How can you reach out?

_____

_____

_____

_____

_____

_____

_____

_____

_____

_____

_____

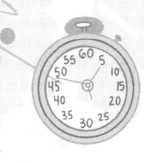

Hospitality

*M*y house isn't big enough. My house isn't clean enough. My furniture is old. My kids are rowdy. I'm not a good enough cook. I don't have time.

This is a partial list of excuses I've used before so that I wouldn't have to be hospitable. But hospitality is more than a meal prepared. It's more than nice dishes and a tidy living room. It's more than being able to manipulate your cloth napkins into cute bunnies or fancy folds.

Growing up in a large family did not lend itself to many dinner invitations, but there was one family in our church that was brave enough to have the entire Anderson clan, all six of us, over for dinner periodically. The Chupp family. I always thought their house was eccentric; it was a mid-century modern, with a spiral staircase leading the way to a library loft. In contrast, the basement served as a teen hangout with foosball and ping-pong and books of all kinds.

The Chupps always had the coolest gadgets and games, but it

wasn't their stuff that enticed me. It was the way Mrs. Chupp took such good care of us while we were there. We witnessed friendly, unassuming, down-to-earth, Southern hospitality at its finest.

> Welcoming someone into conversation is just as important as welcoming them into your home.

Hospitality is an attitude of the heart. It's having a welcoming and inviting spirit. It's being easily approachable, friendly, and extending a genuine attitude of fellowship. Welcoming someone into conversation is just as important as welcoming them into your home. Making eye contact with someone can give an instant impression of a hospitable heart. A genuine smile can ease the nervousness of new faces at church. Hospitality is more than breaking bread.

I heard someone say one time, "My husband and I are not easily impressed," and I thought, "What a shame." How much we miss when our hearts are not hospitable toward others. Spending time in fellowship and getting to know one another on a deeper level creates an atmosphere of trust and security.

When we grumble about readying our homes for guests, how much it costs to share a meal, or the condition of the furnishings God has given us, we rob ourselves of the joy hospitality brings.

Our stuff has nothing to do with hospitality.

Hospitality can happen at the local sandwich shop, over the phone, or at your job, because it's the heart attitude that welcomes people in for community, friendship, and relationships. It is how we build stronger ties with our neighbors, our church, and our loved ones.

Whether you serve on paper plates or fine china, plastic forks or silver utensils, it is irrelevant. It's the matters of the heart—the kindness, the effort, the thoughtfulness, the realness of reaching out and caring for others—that make a difference.

When I think about how hospitable Jesus is, it makes my excuses seem so small. I see willing generosity in his relationships with sinners; when he washed the disciples' feet; and his invitation to come to the table, to break bread and to fellowship around the Gospel. Jesus is the epitome of hospitality. Let's reclaim that welcoming spirit of love and care for one another.

Stop and Reclaim

Show hospitality to one another without grumbling. (1 Peter 4:9)

Do not neglect to show hospitality to strangers, for thereby some have entertained angels unawares. (Hebrews 13:2)

Reclaim Today

What's your excuse for not showing hospitality toward others? How will you walk in obedience the next time God prompts you to reclaim hospitality?

_____

_____

_____

_____

_____

_____

_____

_____

_____

_____

Unhappy Endings

$\mathcal{S}$ ometimes we don't get our way.
I know, it's shocking.

Sometimes life falls through: the job ends; the kids mess up; the friend fails; the spouse leaves. Sometimes it doesn't matter that we didn't "do" anything. Sometimes we don't have any control.

These are the moments we remember temper tantrums don't end when you turn three. We still pout, cry, and sulk. We may even kick and scream until someone gives us a little attention. We tire from exhaustion, desperate to get what we want. It's what we do. We're disappointed, self-consumed, and angry.

We've all been there.

How are we supposed to handle unhappy endings? The ones where everyone doesn't fall in love and get married and drive off in the sunset smiling? I've wondered this many times, and the only place I ever get comfort is from the Word of God.

Look at these guys and gals from the Bible: Moses, Job, Joseph,

David, Ruth, and many more. Each of them had a set of unpleasant circumstances—things they wouldn't have chosen for themselves if given the opportunity to foresee the future. Yet, they did two things. They grieved, and they trusted. They acknowledged their pain to the Lord. They grieved their losses, disappointments, and frustrations. They cried to the Lord.

> David: Psalm 130, 142, 120, 141
> Moses: Exodus 14, 15, 17; Numbers 12
> Job: Job 7, 30
> Joseph: Genesis 45
> Ruth: Ruth 1, 2, 3

In the midst of their hurting and frustration God sent them and many others a message, "Fear not!"

Do you trust Him? Even with the unhappy endings?

Don't fear the future or the past. Don't fear people or circumstances.

The opposite of fear is trust. Trusting God with all the details of your life is much harder than it sounds. But when you put it into the perspective of trusting him with the details of your eternity, trusting him with the smaller things in life (however big they feel) should be easier.

Do you trust him? Even with the unhappy endings? What about when you don't understand? When things don't make sense? It's hard, yet there is a peace we receive by reading the Bible and crying out to him. Trusting his plan is more satisfying and comforting than if we try to figure things out ourselves. It's not up to us to always know and understand. God wants us to believe that he's taking care of things, even when they are unpleasant, even when the outcome isn't part of our happily-ever-after plan.

Remember, God's love is greater, his reach farther, his hand bigger. His mind and plans are beyond our imaginations. He can handle your grief, your disappointments, and even your anger. But he doesn't want you to stay there. We move from grief to trust because of one thing: God can be trusted.

Stop and Reclaim

You keep him in perfect peace whose mind is stayed on you, because he trusts in you. Trust in the Lord forever, for the Lord God is an everlasting rock. (Isaiah 26:3–4)

Reclaim Today

What unhappy ending are you being forced to reckon with? Will you trust God?

_____

_____

_____

_____

_____

_____

_____

_____

_____

_____

_____

_____

Isn't that comforting? Isn't that just about the best news ever? I'm so grateful I don't have to walk around looking like a forsaken child. I have the choice to walk in newness. Thank you, God, for the giving us fresh clothes to walk in today.

Stop and Reclaim

We have all become like one who is unclean, and all our righteous deeds are like a polluted garment. We all fade like a leaf and our iniquities, like the wind, take us away. (Isaiah 64:6)

I will greatly rejoice in the Lord; my soul shall exult in my God, for he has clothed me with the garments of salvation; he has covered me with the robe of righteousness, as a bridegroom decks himself like a priest with a beautiful headdress and as a bride adorns herself with her jewels. (Isaiah 61:10)

Reclaim Today

Do you have old clothes you need to discard? What are they? How will you get rid of them and adorn yourself in the robe of righteousness Jesus gives you?

_____

_____

_____

_____

_____

_____

_____

_____

_____

_____

_____

Construction Zone

My husband and I have remodeled several homes through-out our marriage, but nothing prepared us for the damage Tropical Storm Imelda would bring to our community and our home. The forty inches of rain that poured on our town in just thirty-six hours was incredible. We felt the destruction of homes, schools, and churches all around us. We were not the only ones. Over 75 percent of people we knew personally were affected.

In the days that followed Imelda, there was a muddy mess to clean up. Disintegrated drywall crumbled, making floors slippery and plastered with gray, chalky mush. Progress seemed so slow those days. People would come and work, but it was at a snail's pace. We were at their mercy. Our understanding of what needed to be done was distorted by our impatience and own lack of construction knowledge.

There's a big difference in picking out paint colors and re-building a house. Much of the costly repair work was behind walls that no one would ever see. The rebuild depleted us of our desire to ever renovate again.

If you've ever been reshaped and remolded for God's use, then you know how it feels. It can be a mess. Dealing with sinners like us can be messy. We all come to Jesus with our own baggage, our addictions, idols, and preferences. We all start somewhere. Usually that place is dark and dingy, full of the mess of our bad decisions.

> We all come to Jesus
> with our own baggage,
> our addictions, idols,
> and preferences.

Progress can seem so slow as we learn God's way of living a reclaimed life. Chances are, you'll be surprised by the work that needs to be done. It can be hard work. Self-control, humility, and discipline are vital to our walk of faithfulness with the Lord. We might not realize a weak area that needs to be repaired until the Holy Spirit reveals it.

Others may never appreciate some of the work that needs to be done. In fact, many of them won't understand it. They won't know how dedicated we've been to learning how to be joyful, forgiving, or peaceful.

Let's face it. In a walk with Christ, we are constantly under construction. He's making us into who he wants us to be, if we are willing.

If you're like me though, sometimes I struggle against these beautiful changes he wants to make, thinking my way, my construction, is better. Like many of my construction projects, the finished product might not look the way I anticipated. But if it's God's way, I need to trust it's the best way. I'm thankful that God is patient and willing to work with me again and again. He's the Master Foreman, and until he returns, he's not finished with me yet!

Stop and Reclaim

Being confident of this, that he who began a good work in you will carry it on to completion until the day of Christ Jesus. (Philippians 1:6 NIV)

Reclaim Today

What uncomfortable change is God asking you to make? Surrender that area to the Master today.

_____

_____

_____

_____

_____

_____

_____

_____

_____

_____

_____

Embracing Change

God's plans for us aren't just good. They are holy, sanctified—set apart for God's glory. Many times those plans feel uncomfortable, because holy is so foreign to our society today. There may be sacrifice, hard times, and standing alone, but isn't that what holiness is all about? Isn't holiness reshaping me—taking all this worldliness (that I don't even know I've embraced) and reworking, pruning, and changing me to be like him? Like Jesus?

God has holy plans for us. He formulated this plan long before we were born. The baffling concept that living a holy life could be the only way we are truly happy in this world contradicts everything you might know about joy, peace, and contentment. If you're searching for real meaning, friend, it's only found in holy living. Holiness is a matter of the heart. It's your motives and your actions wrapped up in one package.

I was in high school when I realized that you could do all the right things on the outside but resemble a playground for the devil on the inside. I was a good kid, but good doesn't equal holiness. I helped in our church bus ministry, played the piano for church services, and modeled respect to my parents. On the inside I was weak and had succumbed to temptations to do things that, if found out, would have embarrassed me. Thanks be to God that I also have a weak stomach and don't deal well with guilt. It didn't take too many nights out with the wrong crowd before I knew I could never live this way.

> . . . you could do all the right things on the outside but resemble a playground for the devil on the inside.

When our relationship with Christ is nurtured, the sanctification process of drawing us into a deeper relationship with Christ begins. Sweet moments with the Lord in prayer and Bible study in the peaceful confines of our homes are lovely. But the truth of holy living is that while you need those quiet moments, the majority of the Christian walk is spent wandering these dirty streets of the world. Holiness is foreign there. You will walk alone most of time. It is hard work to live a life of holiness.

This hard life of holiness is also where you will be safest and happiest. When we are living according to God's Word, we have the assurance that we are in his will. When holiness is our lifestyle, we can be secure knowing that while we are not perfect, God is remaking our lives, renewing our minds, and restructuring our hearts. He is making us righteous. What a privilege to walk with him and learn to live this set-apart life!

Changing our lifestyles, our motives and our hearts is difficult. We are wired to crave things that are not holy. We are natural born sinners. But when Jesus fills your life, though the road may be less traveled and difficult, you are not alone. The Holy Spirit is there equipping you with what you need. Dive into the Word of God when you are weak, and when you are strong. There's a purpose in this holy walk and it's to bring you closer to the one who created you and gave you purpose.

Stop and Reclaim

Little children, let no one deceive you. Whoever practices righteousness is righteous, as he is righteous. (1 John 3:7)

Before I formed you in the womb I knew you, and before you were born I consecrated you; I appointed you a prophet to the nations. (Jeremiah 1:5)

Reclaim Today

Do you feel it's a burden or a blessing to walk in holiness? What behavior could you embrace to walk closer with the Lord?

_____

_____

_____

_____

_____

_____

_____

_____

_____

_____

_____

_____

Wishing and Hoping

*I*t was Christmas, 1980ish, and my wish list consisted of a Holly Hobbie dollhouse and *Little House on the Prairie* books. Fast-forward to August 1988, when I wished for my braces to be off before my sixteenth birthday. And then, later the next year, I wished for a passing grade on my driving test. I remember many times I wished for, dreamed about, and imagined my desires amounting to something wonderful.

Now, as an adult, I wish for healthy kids, a safer world, and for all mankind to know Jesus. The wishing has matured throughout the years. It's more serious in tone, except for the occasional wish for success in dieting, my favorite baseball team to win the world series, or for the laundry to do itself. There are greater, more important things to be concerned with these days.

All the wishing in the world doesn't give us peace. Some people foolishly wish upon stars and look to crystal balls and zodiac signs for entertainment and signs and wonders, but they do not provide lasting peace, because there is only one source for peace.

Hope gives us peace. It is the confidence in a God who doesn't leave us helpless. He gives us a place of refuge to hope with anticipation. We do not hope like the world hopes and wishes. It's not a selfish wish to Santa or a look into a Magic 8-Ball. Our help is not found in things that will pass away. Our help is found is the security of a savior who has kept every promise he has ever made. He has proven his love by making the ultimate sacrifice for us. While the enticements of this world may offer a temporary or shallow substitute for hope and peace, recovering addicts and redeemed believers everywhere will tell you those quick fixes never last.

All the wishing in the world doesn't give us peace.

Hebrews 6:19 says,

We have this as a sure and steadfast anchor of the soul, a hope that enters into the inner place behind the curtain.

This hope behind the curtain symbolizes the holiest of places, where God and man communed on earth. This place is where we can remind ourselves who God is. He is holy. He is worth the strength it takes to anchor our hope. It's a place of humble realization that the privilege of real hope only comes from knowing who God is! There is great peace and hope found in knowing that the God behind the curtain wants a relationship with us. This holy God wants to give us peace and hope.

So, when you're anxious, worried, or feeling defeated, step behind the curtain—that holy place of special communion with God. When your wishing and hoping seems insecure and shallow, anchor yourself to the God who gives real hope. If you know him, you have all the hope you will ever need. You have the answer to the world's anxiety and fears. What a privilege to share this with a hurting world.

Stop and Reclaim

We have this as a sure and steadfast anchor of the soul, a hope that enters into the inner place behind the curtain. (Hebrews 6:19)

May the God of hope fill you with all joy and peace in believing, so that by the power of the Holy Spirit you may abound in hope. (Romans 15:13)

Reclaim Today

What are you hoping for today? Have you talked with God about it? How can you anchor your hope in him?

_____

_____

_____

_____

_____

_____

_____

_____

_____

_____

_____

_____

Number One Sinner

*J*esus is a friend of sinners.

The Son of Man came eating and drinking, and they say, 'Look at him! A glutton and a drunkard, a friend of tax collectors and sinners!' Yet wisdom is justified by her deeds. (Matthew 11:19)

The proud.

The self-absorbed.

The lazy.

The liar.

The bully.

The gossip.

The disloyal.

The manipulator.

The abuser.

The _____.

And such were some of you. (1 Corinthians 6:11)

But look at this:

The saying is trustworthy and deserving of full acceptance, that Christ Jesus came into the world to save sinners, of whom I am the foremost. (1 Timothy 1:15)

No matter who you are or what you've done, Jesus came to save you. He came to be your Savior from your sin, from this world, from eternity in hell.

Sometimes it does a Christian some good to look back at what they've been saved from. Occasionally, a quick trip down memory lane helps us stay humble. My sin sent Christ to the cross just as assuredly as the sins of a murderer, a racist, or a thief. As a stay-at-home homeschool mom, my laziness, my temper, or a bad attitude toward my husband are just as damning as those "bigger" sinners' behaviors and actions.

Our sin sent Jesus to the cross.

My sin sent Christ to the cross just as assuredly as the sins of a murderer, a racist, or a thief.

When I think of the terrible agony he faced because of our sins, it breaks my heart. I was one of the "chiefest." I was the "some of you" he talks about. Some days I need to be reminded. When I am quick to point the finger or cast a condemning look in another sinner's direction, I just need to remember I was right there, looking for redemption when he found me.

Thank you, Lord, for saving a sinner like me.

Stop and Reclaim

See what kind of love the Father has given to us that we should be called children of God; and so we are. The reason why the world does not know us it that it did not know him. (1 John 3:1)

Reclaim Today

Is there a sin in your life that is holding you back because of guilt or shame? Use the space below to confess it for the last time. Then mark the sin out with red pen and write FORGIVEN over the sin.

_____

_____

_____

_____

_____

_____

_____

_____

_____

_____

_____

Grime

*D*ust covered, spiderwebby, dirt laden, and grime covered. That about sums up the vibe my porch and backyard were giving off recently before the gentle fall of a spring rain. There's something about that gentle pitter-patter of continuous rain that washes the earth of its oldness and rinses nature of its filth. It leaves everything feeling vibrant, cleaner, and more nourished.

Do you ever feel like you need your own personal spring rain, a couple of hours of uninterrupted washing away of the world's grime? Where you sit and soak every last drop of forgiveness, grace, and mercy? Where you walk away feeling vibrant, healthier, and more alive than before? There have been times in my life I have needed the rain for refreshment and other times I have needed the rain for cleansing.

This watering from heaven to earth is exactly what we need after days filled with drought. Our own spiritual grime can seem so thick that it takes more than a quick squirt of the water hose to get clean. We need this washing when our thoughts don't match his, when our minds are not his, when our hands and feet are not his. We need this cleansing that comes from sitting in a spring rain, soaking in his goodness, his presence, and his forgiveness.

> Just like the flowers and trees will flourish after a spring rain, so does our own walk with Christ.

This cleansing rain helps us grow. Just like the flowers and trees will flourish after a spring rain, so does our own walk with Christ. The fresh feeling the earth has after rain is mirrored in my own life after I've communed with the Lord and soaked in some of his goodness. What a generous God we have that he would have enough for all of us—that in the middle of any personal drought he can bring the spring rain to provide refreshment, healing, and growth.

I am consumed with the thought that a perfect God would want this sort of relationship with a sinner like me. I know he sees me through his Son, so I am considered blameless, pure, and right. I still cannot fathom what he has done for me. When I come to him to be forgiven, I am washed clean from the filth of this world. I am astounded by his love for me.

When my sin collides with the gentleness of his grace, I am refreshed. I can enter his presence clean before him, sins blotted out and redeemed before the Lord.

Stop and Reclaim

May he be like rain that falls on the mown grass, like showers that water the earth! (Psalm 72:6)

Repent therefore, and turn back, that your sins may be blotted out, that times of refreshing may come from the presence of the Lord. (Acts 3:19–20)

I have blotted out your transgressions like a cloud and your sins like mist; return to me, for I have redeemed you. (Isaiah 44:22)

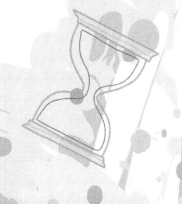

Reclaim Today

Recall a time God forgave you and give thanks for the cleansing power of the rain.

_____

_____

_____

_____

_____

_____

_____

_____

_____

_____

_____

_____

The Power of the Tongue

Proverbs 18:21 says, "Death and life are in the power of the tongue."

I've watched as a person's total countenance changed with another's words. I've been on the receiving end of some of the kindest words and some of the most hateful words. As a parent I've felt the rage that comes from hearing how my child has been hurt by words. I've been defensive when less than well-meaning people have critiqued my family, and I know I've said things that were less than kind and inflicted pain on others. I've been on both sides.

The truth is, our words have power. With power comes a huge responsibility. Our words have great influence. We have the awesome opportunity to breathe life over someone by using carefully chosen words, even in the most difficult circumstances. And that takes time, thought, self-control, and wisdom. Suddenly, using our words just became a lot more work!

Recently after a funeral, a successful musician walked up to one of the women who sang a song during the funeral service. I watched as the interaction took place. Afterwards, the young woman told me what had been said to her. "Your voice has an anointing on it." The words of one musician to another breathed life and encouragement. Seven small words.

Words are necessary. The process of selecting our words is too often rushed and thoughtless. But God's way reminds us we need to be more careful. Less might be more sometimes. Maybe that's kind of the point. Maybe we talk too much. Maybe if we took a little more time, thought, self-control and wisdom, we'd speak more life-giving words and spend less time mourning the damage our words have done.

> Our words have great
> influence..

Weigh your words. Do they speak death or life? There is a consequence to both. Is it worth the consequence? Are my words, opinions, or information so important that I'm willing to divide relationships, hinder unity or hurt feelings? In the past I know I have forfeited meaningful relationships because of my selfish need to speak my mind. Is it worth it?

In a world where our words can be said and shared in tweets and posts, links and memes, we must be sure that we aren't embracing a voice that is not a reflection of Jesus Christ. His words were always meant to draw people closer to the Father God. He was constantly busy doing his Father's business, in word and deed. He is our example. And boy, do we need his help in reclaiming our words to reach the world with the gospel of peace! Let's be careful. Let's speak life.

Stop and Reclaim

Let your speech always be gracious, seasoned with salt, so that you may know how you ought to answer each person. (Colossians 4:6)

If anyone thinks he is religious and does not bridle his tongue but deceives his heart, this person's religion is worthless. (James 1:26)

Reclaim Today

What's the kindest thing someone has ever said to you? Can you think of someone who might need to hear those same words? Tell them today!

_____

_____

_____

_____

_____

_____

_____

_____

_____

_____

_____

Rescue Line

For several days I watched the process on television. One by one, Chilean miners took the fifteen-minute ride in the capsule that carried them to freedom. They had endured the worst circumstances—minimal food, limited water, terrible living conditions. They had survived. As they were reunited with their families, I saw tears flow freely as emotions of thanksgiving, happiness, and relief exuded from their bodies.

I listened to the details of the rescue efforts. The endurance of those who had given the last sixty-nine days of their lives to get these thirty-three men out was remarkable. What dedication!

As I watched, I couldn't help but think about the effort Christ made for us to know him. His own life sacrificed. Sometimes our lives on earth resemble the miners' lives underground those two months—cold, dark, wearisome, painful, and hungry for something. Sometimes the darkness overwhelms the light and our eyes grow accustom to the hurt and pain. We become entrenched in the pit of despair and hope seems distant. The rescue effort may seem so far away that we forget that the rescuer is close by.

I think about Jesus being the one who embraces us on the other side of life. Tears of gratitude stream down my face as his warm embrace envelopes me. Words of thanksgiving and praise drip off my tongue, or maybe the emotions of the moment stifle my verbal skills. Either way, the cry of my heart will always be in utter worship of the one who rescued me.

> I know God is in control. I know the future is better.

Imagine the gratitude those workers felt toward all who helped to rescue them. They claimed hope before they were rescued. When they realized they were actually going to be saved from the pit, the emotions and thanksgiving coupled with hope was enough to get them through. As I grow in my relationship with Christ and realize more and more what he has done for me, I have greater hope. I know God is in control. I know the future is better. When we have that kind of hope and faith, we can't help but throw out a rescue line for someone else trapped in a life of despair.

God is our ultimate rescuer. Occasionally he lets us participate in the rescue efforts. What a privilege to share our faith in God with others so that they can hear of the good news that a God-rescue brings. When we cooperate with God's rescue effort we are part of the big picture of seeing lives reclaimed for eternity. In light of eternity, that is a big deal. Holding the rope, carrying a burden of a friend, shining light on darkness, or cheering for a discouraged friend—these are all ways God allows us to be part of eternal life stories.

Stop and Reclaim

Then they cried to the Lord in their trouble, and he delivered them from their distress. (Psalm 107:28)

The Lord will rescue me from every evil deed and bring me safely into his heavenly kingdom. To him be the glory forever and ever. Amen. (2 Timothy 4:18)

Reclaim Today

Do you know someone who needs to be rescued today? How can you help? Write a prayer for them and then show up to help them!

_____

_____

_____

_____

_____

_____

_____

_____

_____

_____

_____

Doggy Gas and Vomit

School started back that day. Earlier in the week I had wanted to return order to the house, pack all the Christmas decorations, buy groceries, clean the cars out, do laundry, and plan meals. We had enjoyed our two-week Christmas break to the fullest and everywhere you looked, it appeared that unless we tidied up, chaos would ensue when we returned to the rhythm of school.

After being back in the classroom for the first time in years, I knew we had to get a handle on this mess before our holiday was finished or my patience would be running thin! I had prepared the family for the epic post-holiday family clean-up. They were as enthusiastic as you can imagine. Less than thrilled with the agenda, the kids even managed to invite themselves to spend the night away from home with good friends. They thought they had remedied their situation, but, being a reasonable mom, I said yes to the invite and told them that Dad would pick them up at ten o'clock the next morning to get started on chores.

That Saturday we worked hard, but I tell you, even working hard we didn't get it all done. My kitchen table was still covered in Christmas decorations, and the washing machine still had loads of laundry waiting to be washed.

And then Monday morning came. I managed to get dinner in the slow cooker before I left the house at 6:45 a.m. Lunches were packed. I even exercised after school and drank six bottles of water. Things were going along so smoothly—until after dinner.

Tucker (six years old) threw up. He requested grape medicine and saltines. Then I suffered through an episode of *The Flash* with him and the dog curled up on each side of me. And while this might all sound sweet—and I am sure I will look back on this with loving and fond sentiments—I could not get the smell of vomit out of my nose. And right there on the sofa, I snuggled with "vomit boy" and a dog that I'm pretty sure had gas. In that moment it was hard to remember all the good that happened that day—all the things I had done that were good, all the water and the exercise and the lunches I had packed!

> God is on our side

But isn't that just like the enemy? He helps us focus on the bad rather than the good. Helps us to be negative instead of positive. Helps us see half empty instead of half full. Helps us wonder where God is in the midst of the less-than-appealing circumstances. Helps us to question, to think we know better, to get mad, to believe there was a better way.

But we have a choice to fight off the enemy with the Word of

God, or to let the enemy get the victory. We get to decide if we will let Satan devour the good, the profitable, the true, and if we will let him proclaim victory in the places where God has delivered us. We get to make the choices that decide the devil's power over our lives.

God is on our side. We can't let a little vomit or doggy gas rob us of the victories he has won for us.

God is on our side. No amount of laundry or crowded kitchen tables can rob us of the joy of the Lord.

God is on our side. We won't let Mondays, hurricanes, cancer, or layoffs keep us from trusting him.

God is on our side. We aren't going to let temper tantrums, toddler messes, or teenage attitudes delay our responses of gratitude each day.

God is on our side. We will protect our marriages and train our children. We will stand up and speak up.

God is on our side. We will trust. We will pray. We will focus. We will live in truth.

Satan will not win. He will not rob us. He will not kill us. He will not destroy us. He is defeated, conquered, undone by the blood of Jesus Christ. We don't need to be afraid or skittish, wondering if God has this day or any other day covered. He does. End of story.

If your day ends up looking a little different than anticipated, remember that we know the one who goes before us. He knows us by name. He is not surprised. He is familiar with our story. He wrote it. Trust the author. He knows how this ends—doggy gas, vomit, and all.

Stop and Reclaim

It is the LORD who goes before you. He will be with you; he will not leave you or forsake you. Do not fear or be dismayed. (Deuteronomy 31:8)

No, in all these things we are more than conquerors through him who loved us. (Romans 8:37)

Reclaim Today

Have you let the enemy rob you of the victory? Claim three areas where you will be intentional about conquering him, with God's help.

_____

_____

_____

_____

_____

_____

_____

_____

Water Roaches

$\mathcal{I}$ was opening the door to allow our friends to leave after a dinner gathering. That's when I saw them. I don't mean a few either. My back covered porch had been invaded by water roaches—big, long, nasty roaches. They were disgusting and embarrassing. The chill that ran down my spine clearly reminded me of my aversion to most bugs and spiders.

In an effort to rid ourselves of the unsightly creatures, I began spraying bug spray around the perimeter of the porch every day. No sense in doing something weekly when you can do it every day, right? Soon we had dead roaches all over the porch every morning. While equally as disgusting, at least I knew I was remedying the problem.

Our neighbors used to have a dead tree in their front yard. The tree was gray, black, brown—with not a branch of new green life. Honestly, it looked like the sore thumb of the neighborhood. It was at least seventy-five years old. It was enormous. During the last few storms, remnants of the dead tree were scattered all over our yard, their yard, and the street. Finally, one day, tree trimmers came to get it under control. For eight hours they trimmed the dead branches. My yard was covered in tiny twigs and sticks.

All these reminders of dead things—ugly, dried up, lifeless bugs and trees—have me thinking about the things I should let die in my life. As a Christian I am called to die daily to this selfish, fleshly being that cries out to live. I struggle with ingratitude, a complaining spirit, a woe-is-me outlook, pride, and so much more. But these attitudes are supposed to be dead! Whether it takes spiritual bug spray or a chainsaw, they have no place in a Christian's life. It's not healthy! It's downright ugly!

> This full, abundant life in Christ should attract others to him.

The greenness of a life that is flourishing with growth is so much more attractive. In contrast to the dead life, where no one wants to touch or be near the dead thing, the alive life in Christ is something that attracts others. I think about a botanical garden when I think of something beautifully alive. I'd do just about anything to take a pair of gardening sheers and gather a big bunch of beautiful flowers, if they'd let me! I don't know if I would ever get enough to satisfy the craving for beauty! It's the same for those around us. This full, abundant life in Christ should attract others to him. They should want more and more of him because of what they see he is doing in us.

More of him, less of me should be our daily prayer of renewal and surrender. Let's put off those ugly dead attitudes that take the focus off Jesus. Let's have a spiritual pruning and cut off those things that distract us from the good, lifegiving things that God has for us. Let's walk in a life that is fully alive, because we walk with him!

I'm happy to be rid of the dead tree and the gross bugs. They did not bring me joy or happiness. When we dispose of the dead things in our lives, we better understand why the life-giving way of Jesus is so much better.

Stop and Reclaim

But if Christ is in you, although the body is dead because of sin, the Spirit is life because of righteousness. (Romans 8:10)

Reclaim Today

What is something you know is dried up and worthless in your life, but you keep hanging on to it? List it here, and then let go. Give it a proper burial and never go back. Your life is full of life because of Jesus.

_____

_____

_____

_____

_____

_____

_____

_____

_____

_____

Facial Soap

A few years ago my sister bought me some fancy facial wash. It was supposed to renew my skin, removing the dead scaly skin and rejuvenating my skin to look like I was sixteen again! Before receiving this gift, I just used whatever soap I had on hand—and you can only use that anti-bacterial hand soap on the bathroom counter so many years before it starts taking a toll on your skin! And after more than twenty years of just using whatever I had, I noticed my skin wasn't handling it as well as it did in my first two decades. My skin was dry, scaly, and blemished. The wrinkles were more defined, and there were even uneven skin tones (gasp!)

So after a month of using the miracle facial wash, guess what?

The wrinkles, the uneven skin tones, the blemishes, the scaly skin—they were all still there.

Yes, you heard right! It was going to take more than a month to heal the damage I had done to my skin all those years. In fact, it may never heal completely. There will be remnants that only I know about—maybe a scar or a dry patch or even something I cover up with concealer. It's going to be a long, ongoing process.

And that's how it is spiritually speaking. In Romans 12:2 (NIV), The "ing" in renewing makes this word unending or ongoing. It's a continual process of renewing, cleansing, and rejuvenating. It's a habitual practice of hydrating our lives with the Living Water. The Holy Spirit lives and breathes in us. His presence is our living water. His presence, though convicting and comforting and full of hope, renews our minds as we draw close to God.

> *His presence, though convicting and comforting and full of hope, renews our minds as we draw close to God.*

No book, commentary, well-known teacher, or even your preacher can renew your mind. (I know this because I'm married to my preacher, and he's been trying to renew my mind about football, sauerkraut, and professional wrestling for many years!) It's just not possible for someone else to renew my mind. It's a process I have to be in the habit of doing, just like cleansing my skin every day. The process of renewing my mind only happens when I am consistently obedient to the promptings of the Holy Spirit and the commands found in his Word, to clean up the dirty, dry, scaly places in my life.

Maybe you, like me, sometimes find yourself feeling old, dried up, scaly or dirty. Remember renewing your mind is a process that is ongoing. It's not a one-time face-lift that happened at salvation. It is part of our sanctification process. We have not arrived. We are a work-in-progress. One day we will be perfectly complete, but until then, we've got to cleanse ourselves by routinely taking care of our minds, focusing on the things of God, and allowing his Spirit to heal the broken places and renew us.

Just like there are benefits to taking good care of your face, there are benefits to renewing your mind. Romans 12:2, says, "That by testing you many discern what is the will of God, what is good and acceptable and perfect." That's a benefit none of us can afford to miss.

Disclaimer: I have nothing against antibacterial soap! When used properly it serves a great purpose—just like books, speakers, preachers, and your mom's advice. It's when we place our trust in those things and depend on them to renew us, that we buy into the lie that something other than Jesus can do that job. Only Jesus truly renews.

Stop and Reclaim

Do not conform to the pattern of this world, but be transformed by the renewing of your mind. Then you will be able to test and approve what God's will is—his good, pleasing and perfect will. (Romans 12:2 NIV)

Reclaim Today

Are you listening to your friends or your parents or your counselor more that you are listening to God? How can you be sure that the influences in your life aren't just adding to your troubles? Find two verses to help with your struggles and walk in those truths. If your friends, parents and counselors match up to God's Word, then keep them close. Otherwise look for new influencers.

_____

_____

_____

_____

_____

_____

_____

_____

Four-Year-Old Faith

I pray. I pray off and on all day. I need it. It's something that I do for myself, my family, others who I care about, and sometimes, complete strangers.

Years ago, when I was teaching preschool, one of my four-year-old students came to the reading group table. When I looked at her face, I could tell something was wrong. Unsure of what it was, I asked her if she was OK. She shook her head, and big alligator tears rolled down her face. Her big brother had undergone surgery earlier in the week, and she was concerned. I listened and teared up a bit myself as she shared her worries the way only a four-year-old can. Then she said, "Can we stop and ask Jesus to make him better?" Bingo. Yes. Let's do it.

So we prayed. She took a turn praying, and even the little boy sitting at the table with us joined as we bowed before the wonderful, compassionate Savior that knows all about big brothers and little sisters. At that crescent-shaped table I experienced the amazing peace that comes from bringing your hopes and dreams and cares and concerns before the only one who has the power to really change anything at all.

> *Today's lesson from a preschooler: leave your worries with the final words of a prayer.*

In beautiful four-year-old fashion, as soon as the amen was said, she was ready to do her reading. Her cares tucked behind her dark brown eyes. She had talked to Jesus, and she was ready for the next big thing, reading groups. I thought to myself, *That's how it should be. Bring your concern, pray about it, get up and go on . . . leave it with God . . . embrace the peace he gives and get on with things.*

Why do we make it so complicated? Why don't we have four-year-old faith? Where is our innocence in believing he's got it under control? I'm not sure. All I know is that day's little lesson was for the teacher in the class, not the students. The way children trust and have faith is beautiful and refreshing. Perhaps that is why Jesus welcomed them into his circle and why he requires that child-like faith for salvation. Their total trust that God will take care of things captivates the heart of God and leaves me wanting to walk in that same faith and trust.

So, here's today's lesson from a preschooler: leave your worries with the final words of a prayer. Get up. Go on. And when you get overwhelmed again, repeat.

Thanks for the lesson, Lord.

Stop and Reclaim

Do not be anxious about anything, but in everything by prayer and supplication with thanksgiving let your requests be made known to God. (Philippians 4:6)

Reclaim Today

What do you need to leave at the reading table?

_____

_____

_____

_____

_____

_____

_____

_____

_____

_____

_____

The Pit

I woke up thinking about Jonah today. His story duplicates much of my own—knowing the right thing to do, and yet somehow thinking I can outsmart God, buy a ticket to someplace else, get on a boat (where surely God won't find me), cause a big mess (storm), get thrown overboard, and then have a heart-to-heart with God.

It's easy to get caught up in all the regrets, the past mistakes, the roads less-traveled, the lists undone, the money wasted, the time released. Just like Jonah—all those things that we know we should've and could've done, all those commands from God that we ignored, all those things that would have brought him glory that we ignored for our own selfish ways—it's easy to get bogged down in the reflection of failure we see when we look in the mirror. And that's what the enemy wants.

But the truth is, the Lord my God has brought my life up from the pit. Even without being spit out of the belly of the big fish,

Jonah knew God had brought him up from the pit. He claimed the promises that he already knew about his God, while he was at the lowest point of his life—in the churning belly of the nasty fish. He remembered what God had done for him in the past. He remembered the constant God, the faithful God, the one who was strong enough to bring his life up from the pit.

I think that's my defense these days—remembering who God is, what he's done in the past, and recalling how he has brought my life up from the pit. I can rejoice in the faithfulness of a God who isn't finished with me, who has a plan for this life, who loves me.

Isn't that the greatest gift? His love? It encompasses every other attribute he has: his grace, his forgiveness, his compassion. It's that love that brings my life out of the pit. It's that love that helps me look forward instead of backward, and it's that love that gives me hope that he has a plan for my future, just like my past. He's already done so much with my life, I can't imagine what else he has in store.

It's that love that brings my life out of the pit.

That belly of the fish isn't a place I want to go back to. That's not where God intends his redeemed, reconciled, justified children to live. So, I'm rejoicing in my rescue from the pit and pray that God will keep my heart and mind fixed on his Son, his love, and his plans for the future.

Stop and Reclaim

Yet you brought up my life from the pit, O Lord my God. (Jonah 2:6)

He has redeemed my soul from going into the pit, and my life shall look upon the light. (Job 33:28)

He drew me up from the pit of destruction, out of the miry bog, and set my feet upon a rock, making my steps secure. (Psalm 40:2)

Reclaim Today

God didn't design you for the belly of the big fish. When you are tempted to go your own way, what are some truths from Jonah's story that will help you make better decisions?

_____

_____

_____

_____

_____

_____

_____

_____

_____

_____

Ugly Houses

You ou may have seen those commercials on TV that say, "We buy ugly houses!" Sometimes the house will look worn down on the outside, or the inside might need updating. Sometimes the bones might be infested with termites or the plumbing might not be up-to-date. Investors come in, offer a certain amount of money for the property, and the owners decide to take the deal or not.

Just yesterday I was driving down the road and saw one of the local signs for "We buy ugly houses." Having bought and restored two one-hundred-year-old homes in my lifetime, the thought immediately struck me in rebellion. "Ugly is relative." I remember walking through the "awesome house" (the nickname my daughter gave our first remodel) for the first time. It had shag carpet, musty smells, outdated wallpaper, appliances that needed to be replaced, painting that needed to be done, weak flooring, and electrical that would scare even the bravest electrician. And yet, the beauty of the house, the character, the shiplap, the space, the layout, the vision, it was all there just waiting to be uncovered.

Our journey with Christ is filled with similarities. When he finds us, he finds the weak, the bitter, the sin-infested, the unkept. When we begin our relationship with him, he works on our "ugly house" and things start to change. Oh, it may take some time to clean up the cobwebs and to rewire our thinking, but he does the constructive work, and we are made beautiful and restored in his time.

I needed to be reminded of this yesterday. Sometimes the enemy reminds you of all the repairs needing to be done in your life, and there can be a sense of unwelcomed urgency to Band-Aid fix all our sins, issues, struggles and shortcomings. Jesus isn't a Band-Aid fix. He makes all things beautiful in his time. We don't have to rush his work; we just have to be willing to be worked on and cleaned up as he does the remodel.

> Jesus isn't a Band-Aid fix.

His process is done in love and while that doesn't mean it won't hurt a little, it does mean he only has the best intentions for you. With tools like love, grace, and mercy he takes great care to create a masterpiece. Our job is to surrender our ideas of a perfect house and let the Lord do the work that he knows needs to be done.

As we remodeled the "awesome house" we found issues that we didn't know just by looking at the bones of the house. The process to correct bad wiring and plumbing was long and tedious. It cost us more than we originally planned and when it was finished, unless you knew we had replaced the wires and pipes, you didn't even appreciate it!

Spiritually speaking, if we are honest, the remodel process is pricey. Christ paid the ultimate price for our remodel. His death on the cross for my redemption is a price I could not pay. When I accepted the priceless gift of salvation, I began to understand there would be a price to pay for following Jesus. There would be things that would need to change for me to walk a sanctified life with him. The remodeling of my life for his might be uncomfortable and sacrificial. However, in the midst of the remodel there always comes that moment, where you see it all coming together. There is hope. There is anticipation. There is satisfaction. The same is true as God works on us. He allows us glimpses into his vision. We slowly begin to realize his architecture is beautiful. It just takes time. Eternity will tell the real story.

Remodeling doesn't happen overnight. Hang in there.

Stop and Reclaim

Therefore, if anyone cleanses himself from what is dishonorable, he will be a vessel for honorable use, set apart as holy, useful to the master of the house, ready for every good work. (2 Timothy 2:21)

For it is God who works in you, both to will and to work for his good pleasure. (Philippians 2:13)

Reclaim Today

What condition were you in when Jesus found you? How has he fixed you up? Give thanks for those heart improvements.

_____

_____

_____

_____

_____

_____

_____

_____

_____

_____

_____

_____

Underwhelmed

The January blues, the thick of raising kids, responsibilities, service, church, education, work, food . . .

These are all areas of my life where I have a habit of feeling underwhelmed. Ever been there? You start out excited, in anticipation, and then something not-so-exciting happens.

I remember my first day of college. I was thrilled. I had new clothes and new books. I was out on my own, living in a dorm. I had one thousand dollars in the bank, and the world was my canvas. I thought I knew everything.

I remember our first church job, the excitement of planning youth activities and getting to know the church members. I was giddy with the anticipation of fun youth camps and students surrendering their lives to the Lord.

I remember household remodels that started out so fun, full of hope, new paint, new moldings, new looks. I would pour for hours over magazines and Pinterest and envision the beauty that would be mine.

And then the mundane, ordinary, regular, old days set in. The college tests came. The youth work got hard. The remodel costs were more than expected. Instead of feeling excited and happy and energized, the feelings turn tired and underwhelmed by the project or circumstance. It lacked the sparkle, the shine, the magazine look. In what seemed to feel like a minute, my hopes and dreams were deflated. Reality sometimes presents itself as a cruel caffeine. It's the wake-up call after a night of blissful dreaming.

> *Life isn't all mountaintop experiences.*

But let me tell you something special. Lean in. Life happens on the ordinary days. Beautiful life happens in the thick of the remodel. Projects come to life with hard work and determination. Babies become children and then adults smack dab in the middle of dirty diapers, crazy schedules, messy buns, and driver's ed. Life isn't all mountaintop experiences. If we lose the days spent in the valleys or on the climb, we've lost so much. I've got to pay attention to God's hand every day, not just on the days that are wonderful, overwhelmingly beautiful, and perfectly put together. I need to watch him work on test days, bad weather days, construction days and diaper days.

He's up to something. He's looking down on the landscaping of our lives. He sees the bigger picture. He knows where the next mountain is. And in the underwhelmed and ordinary steps of life, we can trust his skills. His navigation is perfection. We don't need to give up or give in. These ordinary moments build skills and determination and a stick-to-it attitude that we would not develop otherwise. There are beautiful moments to be experienced in the underwhelmed days. Don't miss them because you are wishing for better, easier or more.

Child of God, you cannot get rid of him. His spirit is with us in every situation, good or bad—in the overwhelmed, the underwhelmed, and every tiny place in between. What a gift! As his presence comes along side us in every situation we face, we can be sure he's with us in those moments. Sometimes he carries us, sometimes he walks beside us—either way, he is with us.

Stop and Reclaim

Where shall I go from your Spirit? Or where shall I flee from your presence? If I ascend to heaven, you are there! If I make my bed in Sheol, you are there! If I take the wings of the morning and dwell in the uttermost parts of the sea, even there your hand shall lead me, and your right hand shall hold me. (Psalm 139:7–10)

Reclaim Today

What mundane task has you underwhelmed? How can you breathe life back into ordinary days?

_____

_____

_____

_____

_____

_____

_____

_____

_____

_____

_____

Processing Prayer

*T*rying to understand prayer is one of the great challenges of being a Christian. Sometimes I think of prayer as a Star Trek of sorts, like a prayer beamed to Jesus who then beams it up to God on my behalf. Sometimes I just talk to the Lord and leave it there like a grocery list he can choose to fill or not. Other times I feel like a big mess, blubbering my heart out to God. It's more like a counseling session where I'm lying on the couch, and he's quietly taking notes from his chair.

I don't really have the whole process of prayer figured out. But what I do know is this:

First, I feel better after I pray. There is a peace that passes understanding when you leave your life in the hands of God. Being in God's presence and communing with him brings an inner peace that, while I don't understand it, I can fully appreciate.

Second, I forgive more willingly after I pray. When I realize the great patience, grace, and long-suffering it must take God to manage my own life, I find it easier to give those things to others. I want to be forgiven easily, so why would I withhold forgiveness to those who want it from me? I want God to give me grace when I've had a bad day, or when I've slipped up, or when I've been grumpy. So why would I withhold that same grace toward others?

Third, I sin differently after I pray. Believe me, I still sin. But it's different. I am more sensitive, more careful of the way I walk and talk and live. I still sin, but it's less intentional. I am more cognizant of God's presence when I am consistent in prayer with him. His nearness helps me make wiser decisions and better choices. Am I perfect? No, but I am more aware of his holiness and my tendency to violate that holiness. Walking in closer communion keeps me on my toes and alert to staying in communion with him.

> . . . he designed this process
> and desires to hear my
> voice in worship, confession,
> prayers, and petitions.

Fourth, I worship differently after I pray. When I am drawn into God's presence in prayer, there is no way that I can be the same. When I acknowledge his greatness, his majesty and his sovereignty, humility and awe easily take over. My worship of him is changed from what he can do for me, to who he is.

And lastly, I am more thankful after I pray. How can I not be? I have a Savior who intercedes on my behalf. Unconditional love oozes from a Heavenly Father—a God who cares for me enough to correct me and guide me. He offers a never-sleeping, always-available ear to hear my heartaches, my requests, and my petitions for others. How can I not be more thankful each time I pray?

While this is not an exhaustive list of the process of prayer, it is surely a starting place to recognize the pleasure and the privilege of a prayer relationship with our Lord. I'm thankful that he designed this process and desires to hear my voice in worship, confession, prayers, and petitions.

Stop and Reclaim

For the eyes of the Lord are on the righteous, and his ears are open to their prayer. But the face of the Lord is against those who do evil. (1 Peter 3:12)

Reclaim Today

How do you feel after you pray?

_____

_____

_____

_____

_____

_____

_____

_____

_____

_____

_____

_____

Sorrow

"My soul is bereft of peace; I have forgotten what happiness is" (Lamentations 3:17). Have you ever felt that way? Have you forgotten what it is to be happy? Sometimes we get into a rut. We get immersed in our tragedies, trials, and difficult situations, and we can't even imagine being truly happy again. Our peace has disappeared. We are lifeless, beaten down, depressed, and sad.

I know. I have been right there. An emotional tragedy sent me into a downward spiral a few years ago, and all I wanted to do was sleep or eat. I struggled with having healthy relationships, because I couldn't get past the friend fatigue and hurt I was feeling. I was a mess, miserable with my own company. I had forgotten what it felt like to be happy.

And here in the middle of Lamentations—a whole book devoted to a prophet who was so saddened by the behavior of his nation—I am reminded that without real joy, I will never have peace.

But there is hope. Lamentations 3:22–25 (NLT) says,

The faithful love of the LORD never ends!

His mercies never cease.

Great is his faithfulness;

his mercies begin afresh each morning.

I say to myself, "The LORD is my inheritance;

therefore, I will hope in him!"

The Lord is good to those who depend on him,

to those who search for him.

Sometimes we need the reminder that our happiness isn't really up to us. We can be happy (joyful) when we embrace the love, mercy, and faithfulness of God. He is our inheritance! We get his joy as an inheritance, because we are his children. We can depend on him over and over again. We don't have to believe in ourselves; we can fully trust in him, because we are his.

So, while we might struggle with the hardships of this life, God has made a way that we can still be happy. By focusing on what he brings to the table, we can embrace the truths of his character and begin to claim the inheritance of the joy of the Lord. It is truly our strength!

> We get his joy as an inheritance, because we are his children.

When my dad died, he was forty-five years old. My mom became a widow at age 40. As we stood outside the critical care area of the hospital, waiting for my mom to exit alone, I wondered how we would ever get through this loss. The initial shock and sorrow were heavy. My mom exited through the double doors and all three of her children embraced her in one hug. It was then I heard her whisper, "The joy of the Lord will be our strength." Those words ring in my ears and heart today as I have watch God's strength carry me in every life situation. He has been the source of joy and strength.

I remember back to those days of hopelessness and loss. Those were sad days with little to look forward to. But God was right there, the inheritance papers in his hands, waiting for me to embrace what he had for me. It was nothing of myself or anything in me. It was him. Always him.

Stop and Reclaim

In him we have obtained an inheritance, having been predestined according to the purpose of him who works all things according to the counsel of his will. (Ephesians 1:11)

The LORD is my chosen portion and my cup; you hold my lot. (Psalm 16:5)

Reclaim Today

What's robbing you of joy and happiness? What changes do you have control over that would transform your way of thinking and allow you to experience more joy?

_____

_____

_____

_____

_____

_____

_____

_____

_____

_____

_____

Negatives

With a click of a phone, moments are frozen in time. Instagram has built an empire solely based on people's photo infatuation, and Facebook analytics will tell you that a post is forty percent more likely to get seen and shared if there is a relevant photo attached.

I like how a photo tells a story. You can imagine yourself in that scene or recall what you did. Photos bring back memories of good times and happiness. They remind us of loved ones and the power of a negative developing into something beautiful. It's a reflection of tiny details coming together to make something worth remembering.

Like many teenagers, I suffered through an awkward stage. Those few years of crooked teeth, bad haircuts, thick glasses, and funky fashion made for some interesting photos. Looking back at those photos brings laughter and giggles now. Memories of a shy and reluctant girl in her early teens brings me back to a place of remembrance. God used those times in my life to develop me into who I am today. While still awkward and unsure of myself, God has helped me face fears that teenage girl would not have even attempted to face. He was working even back then to create something worth remembering.

That's life isn't it? It's our story: all the scenes—the good and the not so good, the happy and the sad—developing us into something beautiful. All the tiny details come together to make something that is worth remembering, worth passing down, worth sharing, worth taking a second look. It's the mix of unexpected photo bombers, surprises and "say cheese" moments. All these moments paint a clear picture of life. The negatives and the positives show the beauty of a life well lived.

Perfect pictures don't exist.

Perfect pictures don't exist. There is always something the photographer would do just a tad bit differently. Sometimes the imperfections make the photo beautiful, adding energy and interest, creating an image worth remembering. It's those photos that tell the stories worth repeating—those stories of hope and heartache, blessings, and beauty. Those stories allow us to share the greatness of our sovereign God, because, for those who love him, he is working all those things out for our good. They are being transformed in the dark rooms of life. And that truly is beautiful photography.

The reclaimed life knows that faith grows in the difficult places. What seems negative, even ruined or damaged, serves as opportunities to develop the areas where we lack maturity. The hard places of growth, those places where we must trust what we can't see, challenge us to wait patiently for the beauty to be reflected.

Trust God in the dark. He is the only one who has access to the complete picture of your life. As we experience the things he has for us, we can trust his will and his way because he sees what we cannot see. He sees the broken places, the triumphs, the hills, and the valleys. In the pixels that make up our life picture, he sees what will work best for us. When we do not understand, we can trust him because he sees the bigger picture.

24h

Stop and Reclaim

And we know that for those who love God all things work together for good, for those who are called according to his purpose. (Romans 8:28)

Reclaim Today

Is there a negative situation in your life that you wish was more positive? Has God disappointed you by allowing something dark to happen in your life? Express your thoughts toward him and surrender the circumstance to him. He will bring good . . . eventually.

_____

_____

_____

_____

_____

_____

_____

_____

_____

_____

Robbery

"**I**'ve lost my joy." I've said these words—more than once, I'm ashamed to say. And I'm learning how foolish I am when I lose something that is so important. Like the keys to my car, or my kid at Walmart, or the address of a long-lost friend. Foolish.

I've let people rob me, mean looks rob me, gossip rob me. I've let misunderstandings rob me, ministry rob me, financial distress rob me. I've let friends rob me, enemies rob me, and family rob me. I think you get the picture. I've even robbed myself.

The point is this: I've let these things happen. They didn't just—poof!—happen. They came in and captivated my thoughts, my fears, my insecurities. I let them rob me of that special joy that comes from being a child of God and walking with him, experiencing his joy—the joy of the Lord.

Joy can say, "I love you, even though you treat me poorly. I don't want to treat you that way."

Joy can say, "I will make it through this hurt. God's up to something."

Joy can say, "My peace and hope isn't found in my wallet."

Joy can say, "God will never leave me or forsake me. He's with me."

> Joy can say, "I will make it through this hurt. God's up to something."

The joy of the Lord is knowing that weeping endures for the night, but the morning is coming. The joy of the Lord walks in the truth of God's perfect words. The joy of the Lord doesn't let circumstances dictate attitude. The joy of the Lord helps us walk confidently in who God says we are. And as my friend Rita Sweatt said once, "If you can stand clean before the Lord, you can stand clean before anybody!"

I'm learning this art of joy. It doesn't come easily or naturally for my flesh. In fact, it's about as opposite as it can get. No wonder the enemy wants to rob us. No wonder the world tries to discourage us. No wonder we feel overwhelmed by this journey. Joy is directly opposite of anything the enemy wants for us.

Are you wondering where you left your joy? Find it at the same place you found it the first time. It's the real thing with Jesus. There are plenty of counterfeits out there that will tell you it's found in people, prosperity, and possessions. But I know what is true. At the end of the day, you can have all this world; just give me Jesus. Jesus brings joy.

Stop and Reclaim

Be truly glad, there is wonderful joy ahead. (1 Peter 1:6 NLT)

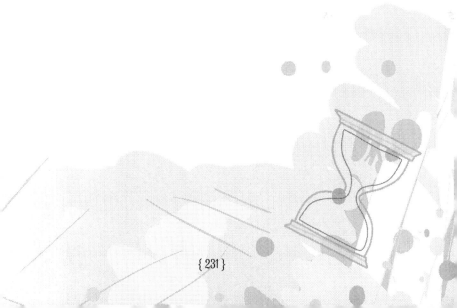

Reclaim Today

Who or what is robbing you? It's time to put the joy thief under arrest. How can you win the victory through Christ?

_____

_____

_____

_____

_____

_____

_____

_____

_____

_____

When Mama Ain't Happy

*T*he old saying, "When momma ain't happy, ain't nobody happy," is a pretty tried-and-true statement. As women, we have huge influence on the temperature of our homes. The climate can change from hot to cold in moments. The way we act and react after we get good or bad news can affect our homes and the people in it for long lengths of time.

If we are taking out our feelings of frustration, anger, and disappointment on the people closest to us, chances are we are not walking in the joy that Christ has made available to us through his death and resurrection.

Real joy is not in job promotions or weight loss.

Real joy is not in good kids or good grades.

Real joy is not in hobbies or friends or a handsome husband.

Those things might bring us happiness—and thank the Lord he gives those things to us to enjoy! Thank him for those blessings and praise him for his goodness.

But real joy is that undeniable, comforting place in your spirit that whispers, *It is well with my soul,* even when things are not well with your circumstances.

When the diagnosis is not good.

When the children rebel.

When the budget is tight.

When your boss is a jerk.

When you are lonely.

God's got you.

Mary found great comfort and peace at the feet of Jesus (Luke 10:38-42). And you, my friend, can find it there too. Mary knew what we know. Sitting at his feet, quietly enjoying his peaceful presence, allows our souls to refocus and be reminded of who he is, his power, his ability to take care of us and his peace that handles our greatest fears. And when you walk away, you can have that real joy that comes from being with him. People will not understand it. Some will question whether or not you're "for real." Others might be waiting for you to fall apart. But God's got you. He can carry you through even the darkest moments, and you can have joy resting in his arms.

There is an old hymn, "Safe in the Arms of Jesus," that brings comfort to me when I am feeling like the world is against me. One phrase catches my heart each time I hear it:

Jesus, my heart's dear Refuge,

Jesus has died for me;

Firm on the Rock of Ages,

ever my trust shall be.[3]

When my heart finds its refuge in Jesus, I am set on a rock that is immoveable.

Stop and Reclaim

Come to me, all who labor and are heavy laden, and I will give you rest. Take my yoke upon you, and learn from me, for I am gentle and lowly in heart, and you will find rest for your souls. For my yoke is easy, and my burden is light. (Matthew 11:28–30)

3 Fanny Crosby, "Safe in the Arms of Jesus" (1868), hymn, public domain.

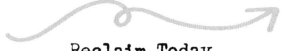

Reclaim Today

Friend, are you tired and weary? Is it reflected in the way you handle yourself? How can you incorporate time with God in your already busy schedule? How can you sit at Jesus's feet like Mary?

_____

_____

_____

_____

_____

_____

_____

_____

_____

_____

_____

The End

The room was dark, except for the small ceramic light in the corner near the bed. Bedtime was a strict 10:00 p.m. with lights out at 10:30. I was fifteen, loved to write, and I had my first boyfriend. What could be more dramatic than the journal of a young girl dreaming her life into existence. Those were the meager beginnings of my writing journey.

Fast-forward to college five years later. I sat in the classroom with twenty-five or so other twenty-somethings preparing to student teach. We were eager to show off our skills in the classroom. For the most part, we were finished with our college studies and would be going into perspective elementary classrooms for the next four months. I sat there listening to our beloved professor share her wisdom and her guidance as she lectured us one last time.

At the end of her lesson, we were told we would be journaling this student teaching journey. We would journal a few times a week, drop our journals off at the inner-school mailroom for her to read over each week, and she would return them to our mailboxes. We would do this for the entire four months.

I wrote of struggles, challenges, triumphs, and cute children. She wrote back, cheering me on, welcoming me into the field of education with each of her encouraging words. And so began my love for teaching others.

> The stories he is writing and has written for you will one day be your history.

And now, twenty-five years later, I'm in a mix of education and writing. And my heart could not be happier. But the journey has not been all roses and unicorns, nor has it been all death and defeat. The beauty of life is the moments that are a mix of both. For it's in those moments, we grow to appreciate the light and the darkness, the beauty and the ashes, the fear and the trust. These pages you've read are just some of the stories of what God has brought me through. And you know what? He's still bringing me through. There will never be an end of things to write about. His stories will be my history.

Friend, the same is true for you. The stories he is writing and has written for you will one day be your history. And all the light and dark colors of your past and future will be the beautiful canvas of your life. The end of your story is not the end of the story.

Your children and their children will have moments of recollection of your life. Why not make these the best moments—the ones that God has reclaimed and purposed for good over your life? Write them down. The silly moments, the joyful moments, the ones that shamed you, the ones he redeemed. Write them for your children and their children, so generations will know the goodness of our reclaiming and rescuing God!

Stop and Reclaim

Only take care, and keep your soul diligently, lest you forget the things that your eyes have seen, and lest they depart from your heart all the days of your life. Make them known to your children and your children's children. (Deuteronomy 4:9)

Reclaim Today

In every story there is good, bad, and ugly. What are your three good, bad, and ugly circumstances that have defined your story? How are you going to make them known to your children and their children?

_____

_____

_____

_____

_____

_____

_____

_____

_____

_____

One-Minute Tips for Reclaiming your Days

1. **Reclaim Structure**: Make your bed.
2. **Reclaim Productivity**: Put your shoes on.
3. **Reclaim Prayer:** Whisper a prayer. Dedicate your day to the Lord.
4. **Reclaim Peace:** Sit in silence for one minute.
5. **Reclaim the Word of God:** Read your favorite Bible verse.
6. **Reclaim Humor:** Ask a child to tell you their current favorite joke.
7. **Reclaim Compassion:** Help an elderly person to their car.
8. **Reclaim Gratitude:** Say thanks to someone whose job is thankless.
9. **Reclaim Giving:** Give a bigger tip.
10. **Reclaim the Church:** Offer to volunteer at church.
11. **Reclaim Memories:** Write out a memory for your children to find later.
12. **Reclaim Parenting:** Tell your child thirty things you love about them.
13. **Reclaim Marriage:** Rub your spouse's shoulders for one minute.

14. **Reclaim Order:** Organize your makeup area

15. **Reclaim Friendship:** Make an appointment to meet up with a friend.

16. **Reclaim Finances:** For three days this week, make your coffee at home.

17. **Reclaim Health:** Stretch.

18. **Reclaim Hobbies:** Buy a coloring book and crayons. Use them!

19. **Reclaim Self-Care:** Put lotion on after a warm bath or shower.

20. **Reclaim Study:** Check out a book at the library.

21. **Reclaim Love:** Write a note to your significant other.

22. **Reclaim Temper:** Take your time responding when you feel your blood boiling.

23. **Reclaim Forgiveness:** Say, "I was wrong. Please forgive me."

24. **Reclaim the Outdoors:** Spend one minute looking at the stars.

25. **Reclaim Fun:** Practice your best cartoon expressions with your family.

26. **Reclaim Mercy:** Let your child off the hook for an offense.

27. **Reclaim Accountability:** Set a goal and be accountable to a friend.

28. **Reclaim Passion:** Peruse the local college course catalog. See if anything sparks your interest.

29. **Reclaim the Goodness of God:** List three ways God has been good to you today.

30. **Reclaim Worship:** List three attributes of God. Think on those things for one minute.

31. **Reclaim the Gospel:** Begin writing out your gospel story.

32. Reclaim Kindness: Purchase someone's meal at a restaurant.

33. Reclaim the Neighborhood: Introduce yourself to your neighbors.

34. Reclaim Initiative: Do something at work without being asked.

35. Reclaim Gentleness: Instead of blowing up about something, treat it with gentleness.

36. Reclaim Faith: Jot down something or someone you've lost faith in. Make one stride toward believing again.

37. Reclaim Grace: Let yourself off the hook for a mistake.

38. Reclaim Gifts: Figure out a way to use your spiritual gift today.

39. Reclaim Song: Make a five-song playlist

40. Reclaim Missions: Drop a quick e-mail to a missionary.

41. Reclaim Connection: Text a fun meme to a friend you miss.

42. Reclaim Spontaneity: Grab ice cream for dinner.

43. Reclaim Power: Speak out loud a blessing over your children.

44. Reclaim Joy: Think about heaven.

45. Reclaim Confidence: List five things God says about you.

46. Reclaim Honesty: Write down how grief makes you feel.

47. Reclaim Dependence: Confess a weakness to a praying friend.

48. Reclaim Patience: Let someone go ahead of you at the store.

49. Reclaim Self-Control: Give up something that is not good for you today.

50. **Reclaim Hope:** Think about how you can prepare your children to be a light in the world they will one day lead. Take one step in that direction.

51. **Reclaim Boldness:** Share a time when God took care of you.

52. **Reclaim Rest:** Close your eyes for one minute (or more).

53. **Reclaim Margin:** Clear your schedule of one thing that keeps you too busy.

54. **Reclaim Hospitality:** Invite someone over. Make a plan.

55. **Reclaim Manners:** Wave to your neighbor, shake someone's hand, say thank you.

56. **Reclaim Respect:** Only use respectful words to describe government officials.

57. **Reclaim Conversation:** Turn off the phone and TV.

58. **Reclaim Faithfulness:** Recommit to your marriage. Let your spouse know.

59. **Reclaim God's Glory:** Give him glory for the good and bad he has allowed in your life.

60. **Reclaim Urgency:** Leave a tract or Bible somewhere someone will find it. Get busy doing things that count for eternity.

You'll find a free printable version of this list and other resources at **www.ginastinson.com/books**.

Acknowledgments

From the time I was twelve, I dreamed of writing stories. Never did I dream they would be stories from my life. This process of writing and recalling childhood memories, blessings, and burdens has been the most challenging and fulfilling process. The work has been long, hard, and, at times, painful. But I have not been alone.

First, I would like to thank my family. Bruce, you have been my biggest cheerleader, giving me accolades, pep talks, and Diet Cokes when I needed them. Our life together has also provided me with plenty of things to write about! Savannah, your unbelievable talent is demonstrated throughout this book in your artwork and doodles. You have been a blessing to work with and a joy to parent! Tucker, I will never forget your challenge to me one night as we sat on the couch. You had a reading assignment, and I needed to write. You said, "Let's see who can finish first." Then we raced to see who could conquer more words in the quickest time. You're a great motivator, and your shoulder rubs were the best after a long day of writing. To each of you, I say thank you. Thanks for enduring the endless fast food dinners, tolerating days of keeping the house quiet, and helping with laundry and chores. You all are amazing!

Thanks to my prayer team: Andy, Jan, Nancy, Kathy, Darla, Sally, and Lori. Your faithfulness to pray for me throughout the last six months has been an encouragement. Thank you for covering me in prayer.

To Felicia, Jaime, Nancy, Sally and Casey, thank you for reading the very rough manuscript and for helping me make this version of *Reclaimed* the best it can be. Your honesty, friendship and love for the Lord and his message radiated through this process.

To my sweet WordGirls, thank you for taking a novice under your wings two years ago and convincing her she had something to say. You girls are the best!

To my professional team: Stephenie Hovland (editor), Michelle Rayburn (interior and cover design), Kathy Carlton Willis (writing coach/mentor/guide/cheerleader), and Savannah Stinson—a.k.a. Savannah Scribbles (graphics), thank you for your expertise and coaching each step of the way.

And lastly, to my Savior, who keeps reclaiming me every day.

About the Author

Born and raised in the Deep South, where accents melt your heart like butter on a biscuit, Gina's gift of storytelling drips off the written page. Her hospitality welcomes readers into authentic, personal, and honest conversations about God.

Gina was raised in Georgia and homeschooled by her parents—before homeschooling was cool. In college, she earned a degree in Education and Bible. She's put that degree to good use homeschooling her own children and teaching elementary school throughout the years.

In between raising kids and teaching, Gina has enjoyed serving with her husband, Bruce, in full-time church ministry for twenty-seven years in Texas. She's been involved in women's, music, and student ministry— serving her fair share of hotdogs and pizza at youth lock-ins.

These days you can find her writing frequent blog posts on her website and contributing to various devotional magazines, including *Journey* and *Pathways to God*. She is also a contributing author to Yvonne Lehman's Christmas Book, *Remembering Christmas*.

A few of her favorite ways to pass the time are crocheting, playing piano, crafting, and spending time with her family at home. She also enjoys browsing small-town markets and fairs.

You can connect with Gina on all her social media outlets:

Website: www.ginastinson.com
Facebook: www.facebook.com/reclaimingeveryday
Twitter: twitter.com/ginastinson72
Instagram: www.instagram.com/reclaimingeveryday
Pinterest: www.pinterest.com/gmastinson
Or e-mail her at: gina@ginastinson.com

Made in the USA
Columbia, SC
30 October 2020